W9-AHE-767

PLANTATION

JESUS

"*Plantation Jesus* is a healing triumph. It exposes white Christian supremacy with fearless urgency. Then it invites broken believers to dare dismantle the worship of racism in exchange for surrender to the reconciling Christ. A courageous call; may all God's people respond in kind."
—*Patricia Raybon, author of* My First White Friend

"*Plantation Jesus* provides a raw, unflinching, and yet ultimately hopeful survey of white supremacy in the church, complete with stories, conversation starters, and practical ideas to help turn conviction into action. A must-read for those ready to confront racial bias in their church and in their lives but aren't sure where to start."
—*Rachel Held Evans, author of* Searching for Sunday *and* Inspired

"I've long felt that churches, filled with people of faith, ought to be the vessels within which the difficult, transformative conversations about race could be held. Yet for the most part, this has not been the case. *Plantation Jesus* boldly shows us why not, and then shows us a path forward. Read this book. Then get busy."
—*Thomas Norman DeWolf, executive director of Coming to the Table and author of* Inheriting the Trade

"*Plantation Jesus* is a unique book that is real and raw about the challenging nature of conversations about race, ethnicity, faith, and the role of the church. The examples and stories provide a practical view of the long-term implications of the church when it unwittingly perpetuates racism. *Plantation Jesus* also provides hope that an authentic view of Jesus can reemerge if people are willing to have the difficult conversations."
—**Kyle Ray**, *lead pastor of Kentwood Community Church*

"*Plantation Jesus* is a well-researched and straightforward work that will contribute to the dismantling of racism if readers will heed the authors' words. . . . Please read this book, give a copy to somebody in your church, and then put the words into practice."
—**Dennis Edwards**, *senior pastor of Sanctuary Covenant Church*

"America is in deep trouble. White supremacy should not be the guiding principle of an enlightened society, and people of faith need to be at the forefront of changing the paradigm, just as they were during the periods of abolition and civil rights activism. The only way to transcend the past is to confront it honestly, and *Plantation Jesus* is a powerful guide for doing just that."
—**Sharon Leslie Morgan**, *coauthor of* Gather at the Table *and founder of Our Black Ancestry*

"Skot Welch and Rick Wilson imagine a church that floods both sanctuary and streets with Christ's love. Anything less would be a failed life. *Plantation Jesus* will challenge you. You may not like what it says. But please ask the Lord for help as you read. Then ask Jesus to use you as a neighbor and healer, as one who binds up the wounds of the brokenhearted."
—**Scott Hagan**, *president of North Central University*

PLANTATION JESUS

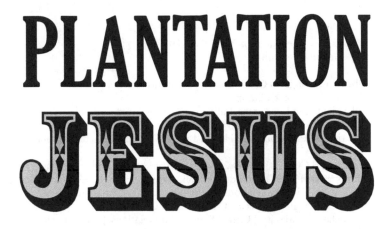

RACE, FAITH, & A NEW WAY FORWARD

SKOT WELCH & RICK WILSON
with **Andi Cumbo-Floyd**

HERALD
P R E S S

Harrisonburg, Virginia

Herald Press
PO Box 866, Harrisonburg, Virginia 22803
www.HeraldPress.com

Library of Congress Cataloging-in-Publication Data
Names: Welch, Skot, author.
Title: Plantation Jesus : race, faith, and a new way forward / Skot Welch
    and Rick Wilson, with Andi Cumbo-Floyd.
Description: Harrisonburg : Herald Press, 2018. | Includes bibliographical
    references.
Identifiers: LCCN 2017057682| ISBN 9781513803302 (pbk. : alk. paper) |
    ISBN 9781513803319 (hardcover : alk. paper)
Subjects: LCSH: Race relations--Religious aspects--Christianity. |
    Racism--Religious aspects--Christianity. | Race--Religious
    aspects--Christianity. | United States--Race relations. | Racism--United
    States.
Classification: LCC BT734.2 .W54 2018 | DDC 241/.675--dc23 LC record
    available at https://lccn.loc.gov/2017057682

PLANTATION JESUS
© 2018 by Herald Press, Harrisonburg, Virginia 22803. 800-245-7894.
    All rights reserved.
Library of Congress Control Number: 2017057682
International Standard Book Number: 978-1-5138-0330-2 (paperback);
    978-1-5138-0332-6 (ebook); 978-1-5138-0331-9 (hardcover)
Printed in United States of America
Cover and interior design by Merrill Miller

Unless otherwise noted, Scripture text is quoted, with permission, from
the *New Revised Standard Version*, © 1989, Division of Christian Education of the National Council of Churches of Christ in the United States of
America.

22 21 20 19 18   10 9 8 7 6 5 4 3 2 1

To Rick Wilson,
friend, brother, truth-teller.
You are missed.

CONTENTS

AUTHOR NOTE

I'VE HEARD IT SAID that you can see God's heart for you by the people God brings into your life. Such is the case with my "brother from another mother," Rick Wilson (1944–2014). Rick's presence in my life showed me that God not only loved me, but liked me too.

Always curious, consistently open to learning something new, and ever eager to have an honest and transparent conversation, Rick never met a stranger. Through our friendship, he often found himself in rooms where he was the only white person. Yet his desire to display God's heart for the mosaic of God's people made him absolutely comfortable in those settings—even more so than in a room where all the people looked like him and nobody looked like me. "Skot," he would say to me whenever we were together in mostly white spaces, "TMWP." That was his code for "too many white people." This room dynamic actually made him very uncomfortable. If only more of us felt that way: most comfortable where God's mosaic is best represented.

Revelation 7:9-10 articulates the makeup of such a room: "After this I looked, and there was a great multitude that no one could count, from every nation, from all tribes and peoples and languages, standing before the throne and before the Lamb, robed in white, with palm branches in their hands. They cried out in a loud voice, saying, 'Salvation belongs to our God who is seated on the throne, and to the Lamb!'"

This was the apostle John's vision, and this was Rick's vision too. Once, when someone wrote a letter to the editor of our local newspaper about protecting the sacred nature of the Warner Sallman portrait of Jesus, Rick called me. He asked if I had read it, and I said no. I told him that I had to choose my battles carefully, and that although that picture is offensive to me, this letter to the editor wasn't an occasion on which I wanted to expend any energy. Rick quickly responded, "You don't have to—I've got this one."

Because of our relationship with the religion editor of the paper, Rick was asked to be the guest columnist, and he accepted. Rick did his thing. He wrote a response to the original piece, citing history and asking questions of the person who made the initial comments, questions that spoke to the foundations of truth as a Christian. He wrote about the part that racism played in the artist's approach to making the infamous piece of propaganda.

What blessed me most about the article wasn't Rick's spot-on response, or the irrefutable facts, or Rick's anointed understanding of the awful coiling together of racism and church history. No, it was none of those. It was the fact that his heart for me as his friend began to feel what I felt.

It wasn't Rick being completely comfortable with being misunderstood or even shunned by people who said they were his friends, as was often the case, that showed his courage. To me, it was his pursuit of the truth, first as a follower of Jesus and second as a journalist of the rarest integrity.

The completion of *Plantation Jesus*, with the help of my gifted friend Andi Cumbo-Floyd, was a promise that I made to Rick when I visited him in the hospital just a few weeks prior to his going to heaven. This is the least I could do to honor a life so well lived—to let my precious brother's voice continue to be heard until Jesus comes back.

—*Skot Welch*

1

WHERE WE START
Introducing Plantation Jesus

GET OVER IT.

The voice booms from the back of the sanctuary. The pastor has just led her white congregation in a tense but respectful discussion about racism in the United States. They have talked about Black Lives Matter and the Confederate flag. They've discussed the murders at Emanuel AME in Charleston and the tiki torches of Charlottesville. They have shared family histories of loving their black nannies and stories about the grandfathers of friends who were lynched. They haven't gotten many answers, but it seems everyone agrees that racism is a real problem.

That is, until the man in the back, who has been silent with his arms folded for the whole conversation, stands up. "Get over it," he says loudly. "Those people just need to get over it!

Slavery ended a long time ago. Racism isn't a problem anymore. Come on; we even had a black president."

And just like that, the entire conversation comes to a
standstill.

This scene plays out again and again in American churches
today. One person's dismissal of a problem shuts down conversation. White Christians who don't see the realities of
oppression and racism in our country lob the "Get over it"
grenade or variations of it. End of conversation.

Once on our radio show, *Radio in Black and White*, we
did a show called "It," as in "Get over 'it,'" and we encouraged people to call in and articulate what "it" is. We wanted
people to tell us what they thought people needed to forget,
overlook, or dismiss. What did they want all of us to get over?
Did they want us to get over slavery? Racism? Oppression in
general? Or would they delve deeper?

On the show, people offered all kinds of rationale for why
they felt people of color should simply be "past" what happened "so long ago." They talked about how they thought
conversations about these things just make racism worse.
They shared that people shouldn't continue to bring up things
that didn't even happen to them. And a few brave souls admitted that when they said they wanted people of color to
"get over it," they were really just saying they didn't want to
feel uncomfortable anymore. They admitted that they didn't
know how to proceed in the conversation about race without
"offending" someone.

We appreciated these honest answers the most. From our
perspective, people who say we all need to just "get over it"

are actually getting rid of their own discomfort. The continuing racial separation in the United States and white people's culpability in that separation makes them uncomfortable. Asking people of color and others who simply can't "let it go" to "get over it" displaces that discomfort a bit.

A dear friend once told us that telling people to get over slavery is like telling your grandfather to keep World War II to himself. We wouldn't expect him to suppress the stories and experiences of that violent, horrific war. We know those experiences were important to him, and we know they shaped who he is as a person. Why would it be any different with slavery or the long history of racism in the United States? Those experiences built the America we know today; they are important to our understanding of ourselves as people, and they have, in every way, shaped our identities as people in America.

In fact, to deny the history of slavery and its legacy today is to deny something fundamental about who we are. Denying the ongoing harm, trauma, and oppression caused by centuries of slavery is to deny the fact that the image of God within people of color was systematically battered, bruised, and imprisoned.

That's why we can't just "get over it."

Meet Plantation Jesus

Denying the pain of someone else's past or present requires being comfortable with the suffering of others. It's in this space of denial that we meet Plantation Jesus: a god who is comfortable with pain and suffering, an idol who can only exist in oppression and codified bigotry. Plantation Jesus provides a faith-based justification for racism. Plantation Jesus is a false god who lives within systemic and institutional racism, who continuously distorts an authentic Christian message, and who is complicit with unequal treatment for financial gain.

Plantation Jesus has been around since the earliest days of Colonial America. He made it possible for white Christians to participate in and bless the transatlantic slave trade, during which 12.5 million Africans were shipped to the New World. Plantation Jesus blessed the practice of baptism and giving a "Christian" name to captives in chains as they boarded slave ships, as they were stacked like cordwood, and as they were forced to live in their own waste for weeks and months on end. Plantation Jesus' name was on the lips of slave traders and ship owners who named these ships *Madre de Deus* (The Mother of God), *Hope*, and *Jesus of Lubeck*—also known as "The Good Ship Jesus."

Plantation Jesus enabled the wealthy and powerful figures from the planter classes in the United States—which included religious leaders and presidents—to go to church on Sunday while raping and torturing enslaved people the rest of the week.[1] Deacons and elders said his name as they put on white KKK robes to engage in state-sponsored terrorism—the bombings, beatings, murder, and torture—of the Bible Belt's Jim Crow apartheid system. Plantation Jesus was the reason that churches and Sunday schools sometimes dismissed early to participate in the vigilante justice of lynchings, which happened in every American state except two between 1880 and 1968.[2]

As an idol, Plantation Jesus has served a portion of the U.S. population very well. He is a god who sits high on the porch of his plantation in heaven and proclaims that the problems of the people in the field, his workers, are not problems he has any role in creating or solving. This god separates himself from those he views as less worthy, maintaining his superiority by creating distance between himself and his people by using hierarchies and oppression. He does not move among his people. He tells them to use the back door. He sits on his porch and watches, removed from their problems. He is not a friend; he is only a cold and distant master.

In Plantation Jesus' view, racism isn't real anymore, if it ever was. In his world, we need to look ahead instead of "dwelling in the past." Plantation Jesus is a god who believes in racial hierarchies even as he wants to obscure the fact that they exist, who puts tradition and country above love and equality, and who sees challenges to the existing systems of oppression as "troublemaking" or "causing drama."

Plantation Jesus is the god of white supremacy: the system that undergirds the belief that white people are more valuable than others. In many Christian churches, he still speaks. Plantation Jesus has allowed us to brutalize each other. It's as simple as that.

But this thinking—this Plantation Jesus thinking—that wants us to "put our past behind us and move on" is hard to question, much less overcome, because America is a nation built on white supremacy. No matter our race or ethnicity, it's very difficult for any of us to see what is really going on because we are living within a system that, by its very nature, is designed to make us ignore or overlook the inequalities and injustices built into its bedrock.

The apostle Peter realized that being Jewish didn't make him an ethnic elite. He writes, "You yourselves know that it is unlawful for a Jew to associate with or to visit a Gentile; but God has shown me that I should not call anyone profane or unclean" (Acts 10:28).

We need to do the same. It is time to dismantle the power of white Christian supremacy. We need to stop following Plantation Jesus, stop partnering with white supremacy, and stop approving its message. Instead, we must uncover the real Jesus—the Savior who was constantly reaching across divides, bridging gaps, righting injustices. By saying no to Plantation Jesus, we can begin to say yes to Jesus Christ of Nazareth, in whom "all things hold together" and through whom "God was pleased to reconcile to himself all things" (Colossians 1:17, 20).

This is hard and deliberate work. We must first identify racist systems; only then can we begin to dismantle them. That work usually begins with recognizing how white supremacy operates in our individual lives.

SIGNS IN THE SOUTH: RICK'S STORY

I (Rick) never wanted to take this trip. I was sixteen, and a long car ride with my brother and grandparents just didn't sound like anything I wanted to put my days to.

My thirteen-year-old brother, my mom, and I woke up on a steamy, hot August morning in 1961 and loaded into our car as my dad started it for the drive to Breezewood,

Pennsylvania, from our apartment in New York City. Once there, my brother Tim and I would transfer to our grandparents' car for the nine-hundred-mile ride to Daytona Beach, Florida, where we would stay with our uncle Dick for a couple of weeks. Within my self-centered, hyperactive, sixteen-year-old mind, *nothing* sounded appealing about this journey.

"The endless ride begins," I said to Tim as we sat in the backseat of our large '61 Chrysler 300 SE. Tim's blank, tired face mirrored my frustration, and in his features I saw the disgust and disappointment I felt in my chest. Because I hadn't passed my New York State driving test, we would be stuck with two drivers who were well into their sixties and not likely to break any land speed records. I did not understand the teachable moments that would unfold during this trip, moments that were only made possible by being with my grandparents—experiencing life within their pace, lens, and personal history.

When we finally arrived in Breezewood, we met up with our grandparents and, after a quick lunch, said goodbye to our parents. After barely two hours on the road, my grandfather began reading motel billboards, confirming the worst fears of two teenage boys anxious to get to Florida. "Howard Johnson's," he said, "Free continental breakfast— ten more miles."

"Ten miles?" I snapped back in deep teen angst. "We just got started!"

I hid my disappointment poorly in ice-cold stares directed at the back of my grandfather's head. But we were barely across the West Virginia line when the desire to stop for the day was too great for my grandparents. Thus a profoundly frustrating pattern emerged: we started late and stopped early for the next four days, living in slow, repetitive motion. It was like our own version of *Groundhog Day*. "We'll *never* get there!" I'd mutter to Tim, both of us deeply frustrated.

Over the course of our trip, however, I began to adjust to this glacial mode of travel. My grandma's remarkable skill in conversation and storytelling helped. As we passed gas stations with "Restrooms for Whites Only" signs hanging tidily from wrought-iron posts, my grandmother made sure we noticed them. Not only did she make sure we saw them; she made sure that Tim and I understood exactly what was wrong with a society that said black people and white people couldn't use the same bathrooms. When I asked where the bathrooms for black people were, she made sure that I took note of a rough piece of wood that was hand-painted with the word "Colored" and an arrow pointing to a shack behind the building.

As we listened to the radio, we passed by restaurants with the words "Whites Only" above the door. When we stopped at hotels at any time of day we chose, my grandma made sure I heard about how black people could not stay just anywhere and that they had to be careful about where and when they drove here in the South. As we passed through small towns like Florence, South Carolina, and Statesboro, Georgia, she continued to point out the signs: "Whites Only." "For Rent to Colored."

"Separate is never equal, Rick," my grandma said. "Everyone here has a choice: to accept what is 'normal' but legally unfair, psychologically terrifying, and culturally brutal; or to stand against it all as a giant, ongoing crime against humanity. You're going to have to make that choice yourself someday."

As we traveled, my grandma's voice rose and her eyes flashed. "It doesn't matter what they call this," she said. "States' rights, separate but equal, Southern gentility, law and order: it doesn't matter how normal it appears or how moral, right, and Christian it seems to be. The romance of a 'lost cause' or 'preserving our way of life' all sounds so good. In the end, what matters is what's right. And on every possible level, this is wrong. The only way to make that clear is to deal with it personally—everyone in their own sphere of influence—choosing what's right no matter what it costs."

She paused to further strengthen her words. "This 'lost cause' is lost because it marginalizes and ignores the authentic story of an entire group of people. It's terrifying, brutal, dehumanizing, horrific."

"How do they get away with it?" I asked.

"The rest of the country doesn't know," she said. "But that's about to change."

She was right. While most of the country was focused on the Cuban missile crisis and the "space race," the civil rights movement was gaining traction. When the Freedom Riders' bus was bombed in May in Anniston, Alabama, the whole country was forced to understand that the issues of racism in the South were not minor, isolated, or hidden any longer. The tensions of that oppression were about to come to a head, and my grandmother knew it. Her fervor about injustice reached my teenage heart on those long days of travel.

My grandmother didn't understand a lot of things about the layers of bigotry in the North—her home state of Michigan being one of the country's most segregated. I had a lot to learn too. I could not have known it then, but at that moment, during a trip that I never wanted to take, a seed was planted in my heart to follow in my grandma's footsteps.

"BREAK-DANCE FOR US": SKOT'S STORY

I (Skot) grew up as a part of a family that valued community. My multiethnic family shared a huge house with my aunts and uncles in Grand Rapids, Michigan, so I was raised surrounded by men and women who loved me for all of who I was, including my identity as a black boy.

On the weekends, we had big parties that moved through all six of the apartments in that huge, white house. Music filled every room—James Brown, Gil Scott-Heron, Gladys Knight.

Sometimes my mom even let me DJ. I'd spin records and dance those hours away with people having healthy, rich fun. Not only did music fill our home, but I also went to concerts by some of the greatest black musicians of all time—from The Spinners to Rick James to Prince and Michael Jackson. I even got to meet Michael once. My understanding, through these musicians, was that black people could achieve (and were achieving) great things in our society. I wasn't oblivious to the prejudice and bigotry in the United States. But because of my family and our love of music, as well as our strong appreciation for history, reading, and civic engagement, I never operated in a deficit. Struggle was never a key part of our family conversation.

I knew racism existed, but not because I was a victim of it. Despite what Rick witnessed in the South and what was true for other people of color in the North, racism wasn't something that was happening to me. I was part of a family that was moving against racism. We were socially conscious folks who were working against our society's prejudices and bigotry. My family members went to marches and told me all about them. We were advancing the cause to end racism. I was aware that we were coming against something. But the personal experience of racism? That just wasn't my experience, even as I grew up in the racial turmoil of the 1960s and '70s. I grew up knowing that black is beautiful and being black is a strength.

When I was eighteen, I encountered, maybe for the first time, racism in a personal way. I was traveling with Up with People, an international performance group, and we had just arrived in northern Germany. I was assigned to stay with a host family, and they met me at the airport and greeted me warmly. They seemed friendly, and I was glad they spoke a little English and that I spoke a little German.

When we arrived at their home, their teenage children told me they wanted to show me something in the basement. There, I found cardboard laid out on the floor in the center of the room. My hosts smiled at me and then at the cardboard. I looked at them and then at the cardboard.

Finally, one of them said, "We want you to break-dance for us."

I cannot even imagine what my face looked like in that moment. I told them I didn't know how. At first I couldn't even figure out why they had thought I would. Then I realized that they assumed all African American men knew how to break-dance.

I'm not sure what they thought about my "failing to represent." But from that moment on, they spoke only in German except when absolutely necessary. Sometimes, I could tell they were making snide comments about me, because they would look at me and then make faces at each other. It was one of the weirdest experiences of my life. I could not wait to get back to the bus and return to the normal life of traveling with my friends from all over the world.

I can't say that this was definitely racism—but I can't say it wasn't, either. It was definitely stereotyping, and it definitely made me more aware of the way people prejudge others because of assumptions about ethnic identity.

IF THE SLAVES ARE FREE: SKOT AND RICK

Our childhood experiences definitely shaped who we were as adults and our understanding of race and racism. This is, of course, the case for every American. What we learn as children is foundational to what we believe and accept as adults. And this is true in the church just as it is in every other part of our lives.

It was our ties to the church that brought us together—first merely as members of the same church and then, in time, as friends. But it was our work to understand the racism that had shaped so much of our lives—even when we didn't realize it—that tied us together as brothers.

In the late 1990s, we were both involved at a large church in Grand Rapids, Michigan—Rick as a director of television ministries and Skot as a member and sometimes as a diversity management consultant. One day, I (Skot) was working with executive staff in a meeting that Rick attended. I talked about patterns of racial and ethnic separation that should be obvious to all. "When was the last time you went out to dinner, played golf, or had coffee with someone who doesn't look like you?" I said. "When have you taken a vacation, worked on a project, or even talked on the phone with a person whose skin color and culture is different from your own?"

As Rick reflected later, he quickly realized that he was guilty on all counts. So Rick and his wife, Laurie, invited me and my wife, Barbara, to come over for dinner the very next week.

Over a meal of spaghetti and Coca-Cola, the four of us sat at a table near their kitchen and had an easy conversation about music, our personal journeys, and the hard questions of inequality and racism. Rick asked me a lot of questions, trusting in our shared Christian faith and our mutual commitment to justice. We talked for a long time, and that dinner affirmed—for both of us—that our friendship was going to be easy and real and deep. It was going to be a relationship based on true affinity and love, not something that was ever programmed or forced.

We grew together as we came to understand more about the layered dynamics of racism and the cultural reality of bias and discrimination, and as we began to know and call out the work of Plantation Jesus around us. As our mutual friend Juanita Brown, an educator and colleague, said once on our radio program, cross-racial friendships and partnerships aren't *supposed* to work. But our relationship did work, and it shaped both of us at our very core.

We both eventually left that first church and became members at a spectacularly successful megachurch in Grand Rapids. This church had grown from three hundred people to five thousand weekly attendees in ten years. The congregation was overwhelmingly white. African Americans, Latinos, Asians, and people from other communities of color were very poorly represented—less than one-tenth of 1 percent of the total congregation. At the time we were there, the church leadership was wrestling with questions about whiteness that we couldn't answer. What is at work within white European Americans that has kept systemic racism firmly in place? Why is any kind of conversation about racism so difficult?

Rick was working as the director of communications, and his grandmother's words never left him: "Separate is never equal—you have a choice to make." At the same time, I was privately consulting with the church leadership about how the church could more fully represent what the kingdom of God looks like.

This was the congregation's stated desire: to more accurately reflect God's kingdom in their ethnic and racial makeup. They hired Scott Hagan, a man with a heart for that work, as pastor. Yet attempts to talk about racism, bias, bigotry, and their institutional roots in American history were met with obvious discomfort among the church's European American members. Every conversation on these subjects would survive only for a few awkward moments before someone quickly and intentionally changed the subject.

Pastor Hagan asked us and our colleague Susan Gangwer Ripley—a friend who had been intimately involved in the conversations we'd been having within the church community—to form a group called Mosaic to facilitate the church's stated desire to become a multiethnic congregation. Our job as Mosaic was to educate the congregation about differences in ethnicities, to facilitate conversations, and, in short, to help bring healing. We organized conversations about race and encouraged congregation members to ask questions, listen honestly, and explore their own ideas about race, ethnicity, and difference.

Unfortunately, Mosaic did not last for very long. The congregation ultimately did not embrace the vision. In fact, Pastor Hagan left the congregation in a tide of racialized bigotry that should never be a part of the church of God. The ugly backlash by some in the congregation took the form of open letters printed in the Grand Rapids press accusing Pastor Hagan of loving black infants more than white infants during baby dedications. Racially vulgar graffiti was written on the church property. The previous pastor had nobly recognized the awful and historical social sins of Grand Rapids and had begun to publicly address them before his retirement, but Pastor Hagan's message and modeling brought a new and heightened intensity to the reconciliation experience. The clarity of his theology and the direct nature of his messages created real enemies out of some who had sat comfortably in the church for years. Some would say Pastor Hagan's message failed; others would say God used him to bring a necessary disruption. As an African American with a front-row seat, I

(Skot) would simply say it was incredibly painful to watch, and the reasons these events happened are still alive today in both society and the church at large.

But as is the way with the things of God, Mosaic laid the foundation for the work Rick and I would do together for many more years. Shortly after we left that congregation, Rick approached me with the idea of a radio show focused on these conversations about racism and diversity and acceptance. After serious reluctance on my part—I didn't want to yell at people—we began our broadcast journey in March 2006, when our show, *Radio in Black and White*, was born.

On air, we tried to display and model the patience, grace, and leadership skills that allow people to see what was and is hidden from view—what our friend Tim Wise, an antiracism activist, calls "Racism 2.0": a racism much less confrontational in tone and style than Jim Crow. Racism 2.0 is a racism far more subtle, a racism that effectively flies under the radar.[3] In this codified culture of silence (as Beverly Tatum, author of *Why Are All the Black Kids Sitting Together in the Cafeteria?* and former president of Spelman College, calls it [4]), it became quite clear why the meaningful conversations we had attempted in our last church were consistently shut down. The Mosaic team had not been able to break that code.

One of our guests on the show, Llewellyn Smith, unwittingly introduced us to a concept that would, in time, help us begin to break through that code. Smith, a film producer and collaborator on films including *Eyes on the Prize* and *Race: The Power of an Illusion*, was talking about research for the documentary *Reconstruction: The Second Civil War*.

He remembered reading a series of letters written by plantation mistresses whose husbands were fighting in the Civil War during the winter of 1865, when the end of the war was a foregone conclusion in the South. With defeat inevitable, many of these women were musing about what a postbellum world would look like. One wife asked her husband about life without slavery: "If the slaves are free," she wrote, "does God exist?"

As we heard Smith quote from that letter, we felt ourselves pull up short. If the slaves are free, the woman wondered, does God exist? If the system that gave her wealth, a system that had been long condoned as God's will, disappeared, did that mean that God disappeared as well?

It's hard to put into words our feelings at that moment, on a live radio show, as we received a spectacular revelation of history. The ending of slavery—an institution that is widely regarded as one of the most horrible in human history—would cause a woman to doubt the existence of God. Something was deeply wrong then. Something is deeply wrong now.

This was the moment we came to see Plantation Jesus as part and parcel of our American Christian existence. This was the moment we recognized the face of Plantation Jesus and the ways that he had warped Christian understandings of God's love for humanity.

Rick had first noticed Plantation Jesus on that hot trip through the South with his grandparents. This warped imagining of god was an integral part of what made everything look so normal, moral, right, and Christian there, deep in the heart of the Bible Belt but far from God's heart and mind.

Skot had caught a glimpse of this misshapen idea of the divine in the way that our church shut down not only the conversations but also the people who were seeking to reveal the deeply racist systems in our congregation.

From that moment on, our awareness of Plantation Jesus would launch our passion to expose the worst aspects of racialized religious bigotry—a bigotry that is fueled by ignorance and that continues to make eleven o'clock on Sunday morning "the most segregated hour in Christian America," as Martin Luther King Jr. frequently said. Sadly, racism and religion work very well together.

"Between the Christianity of this land, and the Christianity of Christ, I recognize the widest possible difference," Frederick Douglass wrote.[5] That difference is the heart of this book. We want to graciously and decisively present a Christocentric message. To do so, we may need to break through layers of delusion and denial. This process can be painful, and we invite you to face that pain rather than turning back to easy answers or feel-good responses that pretend injustice away.

Beyond Plantation Jesus, the real Jesus awaits. The true gospel message is fully compatible with the "Christianity of Christ," in Douglass's words, and fully at odds with the "Christianity of this land," laden as it is with historical and ongoing racism. But there is a way forward, a way forward that pours forth from the hand of Love: the hand of the real Jesus.

DISCUSSION QUESTIONS

- Have you ever heard (or said), "We need to get over it"? What did that phrase refer to? Why do you think it was said?

- How familiar are you with the history of the Civil War? With the civil rights movement?

- What is the relationship between slavery and Christianity in the United States? Is that relationship over? Why or why not?

- Discuss this idea of Plantation Jesus. Have you ever seen Plantation Jesus at work? How or when?

- What do you do when you see your faith being misrepresented?

- When you think about conversations about race and Christian faith, how do you feel?

2

WHY CAN'T WE TALK?
Ten Roadblocks to Real Conversation

W E'VE ALL HAD those conversations: the ones about racism in which we feel that we don't know what to say, we don't feel heard, and we get our feelings hurt. These feelings are often more extreme for those of us who are white, because our society does not require us to engage with questions about race and ethnicity on a daily basis. Our society sees whiteness as the norm, and thus those of us who are white can operate as if race and ethnicity—and the challenges America faces around these issues—are not our problem. Then, when we are brought into conversations about these topics—or when we begin those conversations ourselves—we often flounder and sometimes get defensive. Maybe for the first time we are being confronted with truths that are hard for us to see, not to mention take responsibility for.

Conversations about race and ethnicity can be complex, painful, and difficult. But it's essential that we all join the dialogue. As the two of us have walked into this arena, we have been called race-baiters, cowards, loudmouths, divisive, factless, and failures who don't understand the great commission. While it's hard for us to handle baseless and banal charges like these, we actually have come to think that they're not the worst responses we've gotten.

The worst response we've received is silence. Trying to start a conversation on race and being confronted by white people's silence is frustrating and demeaning, and it can feel as if people think our points and our experiences aren't even worthy of being addressed. We know that sometimes people are silent because they are afraid they will say the wrong thing. But being afraid to say something wrong cannot excuse saying nothing.

Sometimes in these conversations, we resort to or are confronted with statements that arise out of defensiveness and fear. We have found that identifying these statements so we can be prepared to confront them is wise. What follows in this chapter are ten statements that are similar to the "Get over it" line we've heard time and time again. We've gathered them from interpersonal conversations, calls to our radio show, and articles and talking points on various radio and TV programs sent to us by friends. These statements cause conversations to crash because, while they appear to be authoritative, there are no facts behind them. Thus, the dialogue is over before it begins.

Have you ever heard—or made—any of these claims? Let's examine these ten statements carefully.

1. "RACE HAS NOTHING TO DO WITH ME"

One night, we were involved in a diversity training class at a local college. In the beginning of such classes, we use icebreakers that include asking participants what they know about their ethnicity and if their name means something. That night, we were getting somewhat typical responses— Irish, Dutch, German, Italian, Polish—until we came to an older gentleman whose demeanor spoke volumes.

With furrowed brow, clenched fists, and squared shoulders, this white man stared directly at Rick. "I'm an *American!*" he said.

Pausing for a moment, we attempted to pursue the question. "Well, sir, I think we could all say that," one of us said. "What we're looking for is your ancestry. Do you know how your parents or grandparents got here? Where did *their* ancestors come from?"

His body language and response did not change. "I'm an *American!*" he said, as forcefully as before.

Clearly, this man was not willing to engage the question of ethnicity. That question was, for him as a white man, already answered. In his mind, being American was equivalent to being white.

Seeing the conversational impasse, we went on to the next person. But we never forgot his statement, which is built upon both denial and cognitive dissonance.

With profound frustration, many people of color have expressed that race is something they are forced to deal with all the time while white people can choose to ignore any kind of racial dynamics in their "normal" white world. Sadly, the vast majority of European Americans pick that path: the classic line of least resistance. This deep denial was on full display in our diversity class that day.

This man's defiant, confrontational body language and tone of voice—he was an American, and no one was going to tell him any different—demonstrate cognitive dissonance, which is best defined as two conflicting beliefs coexisting within the same person. As America increasingly becomes more black and brown, and as the definition of what it means to be an American changes, European Americans often experience deeply rooted distress that something is being lost, something that they must find again. Statements which suggest that the United States needs to return to its roots of greatness imply that the greatness of America resides within white, wealthy men, because they are the only Americans who have consistently been treated well in our nation.

This kind of belief is both wrong and dangerous. America has never been a land of solely white people. From the Native Americans who lived in this land before European colonists arrived to the Spanish Indian inhabitants of the American Southwest to the Africans who were brought to these shores as slaves: America has never been a nation made up of only white faces. To glorify a limited and exclusive vision of historic America is to deny our true, rich, complex history and to reinforce racial hierarchies that lead to discrimination, oppression, and violence.

Race, ethnicity, history, and culture have everything to do with *all* of us. The more we discover our history, both nationally and personally, the better off we *all* are.

2. "*I* NEVER OWNED A SLAVE"

This statement surfaced during a meeting we had with a potential sponsor for our radio show. As our conversation drifted toward the legacy of slavery in America, a history portrayed powerfully by films such as *12 Years a Slave*, our client offered up the oft-heard familial disclaimer: "But *I* never owned a slave. No one in my family did."

"Neither did anyone in my family," Rick replied to our client, who was also a personal friend. "But the journey I'm on now is to find out just what my ancestors did in this country to directly or indirectly empower the slave trade. That not only includes ownership but also trading, financing, communication, and marketing."

After a somewhat awkward pause, our conversation moved on to other things. But the point was made. Only by going honestly into the past can we understand what we're dealing with in the present and what we will continue to deal with in the future.

Slavery was not an unfortunate, brief, tragic left turn in American history. Slave systems were foundational to the United States morally, spiritually, sociologically, culturally, and economically. Wealthy planters like George Washington, Thomas Jefferson, and James Madison owned hundreds of slaves during their lifetimes and were involved in the mundane business affairs of bondage. Ordinary

Americans—including clergypersons, bankers, insurance ex-
ecutives, and tradespeople—owned smaller numbers of human chattel within the same system.

So, no, we did not start the system of slavery, and we may
not have directly participated in it. Yet across history, the
slave system still reverberates, and benefits still accrue on
the basis of history's divided spoils. As renowned educator
and author Joy DeGruy says, "246 years of protracted slavery
guaranteed the prosperity and privilege of the South's white
progeny while correspondingly relegating its black progeny
to a legacy of debt and suffering."[1] It is this horrific legacy of
trauma that forms the basis of disparities we're dealing with
now. Saying "I never owned a slave" is a disingenuous and
ineffective attempt at dodging responsibility for the suffering
around us. We have to own the ways we've benefited from
its legacy. Only then can we deconstruct what our ancestors
constructed.

3. "Slavery is in the Bible"
Upon this false foundation, Plantation Jesus builds his elabo-
rate system of race-based bondage. The European Americans
who make this statement are sometimes unaware that the
Bible does not actually support them or their slave-trading
ancestors. They latch onto verses like 1 Peter 2:18-20 and suggest that since slavery appears in the pages of Scripture, it
must not have been so bad.

But the enslavement of humans runs counter to the desires of God's heart. This truth is clear from the very beginning of Scripture, when God says, "Let us make humankind

WHY CAN'T WE TALK? / 39

in our image, according to our likeness" (Genesis 1:26). Paul's letter to the Galatians includes one of the texts that speaks directly against the idea that God supports slavery. In Galatians 4:6-7, Paul says, "And because you are children, God has sent the Spirit of his Son into our hearts, crying, 'Abba! Father!' So you are no longer a slave but a child, and if a child then also an heir, through God." All believers in Christ are given the title "children of God." In other words, we are siblings. No one enslaves one's own brother or sister.

Further investigation of the Bible also brings us to passages that challenge the system in other ways. For hundreds of years, Africans were kidnapped and shipped to slave markets throughout the Americas. The United States was one of the largest markets in the world, and slavery made this country very rich in a short amount of time. Kidnapping is never justified in Scripture: "Whoever kidnaps a person, whether that person has been sold or is still held in possession, shall be put to death" (Exodus 21:16).

Or consider how slaves were treated. In America, the treatment of enslaved Africans was horrific and unconscionably cruel. Rape, torture, and murder were a normal way of life for millions caught in what has been called this "peculiar institution." This kind of inhumanity is never seen as appropriate behavior in the Bible; it is never something to be admired and emulated.

Additionally, slaves lived in bondage forever. Since many white people believed that slavery was the "accursed" condition for Africans, once people entered that institution, they could not leave it. (White Christians sometimes referenced the "curse of Ham" or the "mark of Cain," misreadings of Genesis 9:20-27 and Genesis 4:11-16, as explanations.) The poorly translated Greek word *doulos*, which is sometimes taken to mean "slave," really means "bond servant." In the first century, this word meant that service had a beginning and end. Nothing in the Bible defines or endorses slavery by ethnicity or race in perpetuity.

Finally, masters saw enslaved people as property, not human beings. They were viewed as chattel, property, exactly the same way that horses, cows, and chickens were seen. They were investments that had to produce to earn their keep. In practical terms, human chattel was used as collateral for debts, was put on a sliding scale of depreciation as slaves aged, and was insured against loss.

Reflecting on an experience from when he was eleven years old, Frederick Douglass described the process of "valuation" and division of property when a planter died without a will:

> We were all ranked together [in a field] at the valuation. . . . There were horses and men, cattle and women, pigs and children all holding the same rank in the scale of being, all subjected to the same narrow examination. . . . At this moment, I saw more clearly than ever the brutalizing effects of slavery upon slave and slaveholder.[2]

In no way does the Bible condone the valuing of human beings as property. That very notion belies the central tenets of Christianity. This kind of brutality finds no support in Scripture, where again and again we are reminded that God loves human beings as God's children. Instead, this system is an American brand of bondage. American slavery was unique in its cruelty. It was a giant crime against humanity.

4. "SOME PEOPLE WERE NICE TO THEIR SLAVES"

This seemingly innocuous statement is deceptively layered in what sociologist James Loewen calls "the magnolia myth." This myth maintains that "slavery was a social structure of harmony and grace that did no real harm to anyone, white or black."[3] The prevailing narrative that makes this believable is the well-worn picture of slavery as benevolent paternalism: happy slaves being cared for by humane plantation patriarchs in the bucolic grandeur of rolling hills and soaring antebellum architecture.

In this narrative, "Big Daddy," the slaveholder, always knew best. His relationship with his slaves is something like that of a parent with a child. This is the image of slavery that celebrity chef Paula Deen was calling forth when she made her painful comments about wanting a "really Southern plantation wedding," complete with black waiters playing the part of slaves.[4]

It is not hard to break down this idea—that slavery was a mostly humane institution—as misguided, inaccurate, and dangerous. First, while it is true that slave owners exhibited varying degrees of brutality against the people they enslaved, the vast system of slavery was unimaginably cruel by nature. When bondage is practiced by its main players, no matter how "good" life may have seemed relatively, slavery was still a system that denied people basic human freedoms and dignity, and there was nothing "good" about that practice. Enslaved people are caught in a world of forced labor in perpetuity. They can't leave. It's hard for us to imagine a slave's world, in which they were not allowed to step foot from a particular area without written permission from a person who could buy and sell them at his or her whim. But that was the truth of slavery, even when there was nary a whip in sight.

For this reason, many, many enslaved people were determined to leave or to fight for their freedom. People who are content and happy do not try to leave or plan revolt. In the prime years of slavery in the 1800s, more than one hundred thousand people used the Underground Railroad as a means of escape.[5] Additionally, enslaved people often planned uprisings. No fewer than fourteen armed insurrections occurred in the Americas between 1663 and 1859.[6]

Put simply: slavery is never nice, no matter how it is practiced or who is driving the business of bondage. The more we research, the more we realize how inhumane American chattel slavery was on a personal level. Our friend Sharon Morgan, a genealogist and the founder of Our Black Ancestry, has examined her own family extensively. "I share the pathos of *generations* of people—my people—kidnapped, chained, whipped, crippled, violated, and traumatized in every possible way," she says. "Slave masters reduced themselves and their prey to a level of barbarity that defies imagination, unleashing a vicious cycle of violence that informs our society unto this very day. I cannot fathom the cognitive dissonance of these men (and their consort wives) who did what they did and justified it with the word of a god I do not know."[7]

There he is again: Plantation Jesus. No, nothing about the system of enslavement was benevolent or good. Not a thing.

5. "I DON'T SEE COLOR, ONLY PEOPLE"

Have you ever known someone who is truly colorblind? We had a friend who struggled with colorblindness; to compensate, he asked his wife to help him pick out his color combinations as he dressed for work. But we always knew those rare occasions when she was out of town. On those days our friend would come to church in some of the most wildly out-of-sync colors you could imagine. Though we would tell him how his outfit looked to us, and then laugh with him, we knew that he had a challenging condition.

How, then, have we come to lift up "colorblindness" with regard to race as an asset and not a liability? As something to strive for rather than a disability? White people like the way the idea—being blind to someone else's skin color—makes them feel about themselves, as if they've "risen above" such categories. But in reality, colorblindness with regard to race is a lie. Children as young as six months old identify differences in people's skin color.[8]

People of color see through this metaphor whenever white people use it, and they don't buy what's being sold: a high-minded ideal that overlooks both the painful parts and the rich cultural experiences of people who are not white. Moreover, such a claim—"I'm colorblind"—is based on the idea of white normalcy and is dismissive of the very real experiences of people of diverse ethnic identities. As more than one person of color has said, "If you don't see my ethnicity, you don't see me."

In August 1963, Martin Luther King Jr. said, "I have a dream that my four young children will one day live in a nation where they will not be judged by the color of their skin but the content of their character."[9] For more than fifty years, debate has centered on the meaning of these words. Unfortunately, the idea that has won the day is that King was holding out the "ideal" of being racially colorblind. In actual practice, this idea is untenable and deceptive. Racial disparities tell us that such colorblindness is not a fact. We *all* see color!

As an example, let's consider our criminal justice system. By the time black men reach the age of twenty-three, 49 percent of them have been arrested.[10] The United States currently imprisons more people than any other country in the world. Although we represent just 5 percent of the world's population, we incarcerate 21% more people than any other country in the world, and of those people incarcerated, 56% of them are African American or Latino (as compared to the 32% of the general population that is made up of African American or Latino people).[11] Consider the deaths of Michael Brown, Freddie Gray, Sandra Bland, Tamir Rice, Eric Garner, Rekia Boyd, Walter Scott, and the dozens of other unarmed African Americans who have been killed at the hands of police officers or who have died in police custody. Does this evidence give you the impression that those managing the criminal justice system are truly colorblind?

Or think about the banking industry, where small business, home improvement, and mortgage loans originate. According to the Urban Institute, "For every $6 white people have in wealth, black people have $1."[12] The banking system favors white people in every decision, and thus contributes to a great disparity in wealth in our nation.

Racial disparities like these tell all of us that, in practice, we all see color. We're not colorblind. Instead, we're blind when we think that we don't see color.

6. "WE'RE ALL AMERICANS"

This statement crashed a conversation with a friend of ours about the differences in experience between whites and blacks in American history. Our friend lived in one of western Michigan's most affluent suburbs and had no contact at all with anyone other than white people. Yet his statement— "We're all Americans"—claimed that everyone's experience of America was the same as his experience as a white, upper-middle-class man. Given his economic and racial isolation, he couldn't possibly know if all Americans were treated equally, as his statement implied. But his refusal to own his own ignorance and his dismissal of experiences that did not match his own were instantaneous. His response was almost instinctual, and was rooted in his desire to *not* see what didn't support his own experience. He preferred to stay within his own bubble of racial and economic privilege rather than acknowledge that others might have experiences different from his. His experience wasn't that of someone quintessentially American.

In her influential essay "White Privilege: Unpacking the Invisible Knapsack," scholar Peggy McIntosh writes about the experiential side of racial disparities. She argues that white people in American culture are perceived as more valuable and less threatening than those who share the same citizenship and birthright in the United States but have a darker skin tone. This is the fundamental root of white privilege and the systems of white supremacy. As McIntosh contends, white people can choose to be in the company of their own race most of the time. In contrast, black and brown Americans are forced to interact in a dominant culture that has little contact with or understanding of them. White Americans can often purchase housing in an area they can afford and in which they want to live. Americans of color are often trapped in ghettos and denied access to quality neighborhoods even when they have the means to live there.[13]

As McIntosh points out, white Americans can shop alone and be confident that they will not be harassed, bothered, and immediately placed under suspicion. Black and brown Americans are quickly perceived to be a security risk in all kinds of retail venues and experience all the trouble connected with shopping while black (SWB).

White Americans can turn on their television sets or look at newspapers and magazines and see their ethnicity widely and well represented. Black and brown Americans are most often depicted in mug shots and perp walks that reinforce a stereotype of them as predatory, threatening, and dangerous.

When white Americans are told about "national heritage" and "civilization," they are taught that their ethnicity had everything to do with making the United States what it is. Black and brown people and their stories are absent from this master narrative. White Americans don't have to have "the talk" with their children about the realities of systemic racism. Black and brown Americans have to teach their children how to navigate the treacherous thicket of structural inequality.

As these few examples out of thousands show, all Americans are *not* walking together on level ground. Our American experience is not framed in equality but instead rests fully on systems that are unequal. A huge experiential gap—between black and white—is built into almost every structure of American society. Yes, we are all Americans. But our identity as such says very little about the daily details of our lived experience.

7. "WE JUST NEED TO TAKE BACK OUR COUNTRY"

When presidential candidate Donald Trump selected his 2016 campaign slogan, "Make America Great Again," he was speaking into a narrative of reconquest, one harking back to the way that European Americans came to territories then inhabited by Native peoples. His campaign was successful at least in part because so many Americans believe in the myth of a supreme white America. "We just need to take back our country," many say.

When we first heard this statement, several questions came to mind. First, who took your country from you and where did they put it? And second, if you take it back, what are the rest of us going back to? It's hard to place "retaking your country" in the context of history when high-sounding ideas like Manifest Destiny justified the genocide and the "civilization" of Native peoples. Just *who* took what from *whom*? It's a legitimate question.

A pastor friend once asked this question in this way: "If you could, what part of American history would you want to relive?" For white people, a lot of choices exist—colonial days, the antebellum South of the nineteenth century, the Roaring Twenties. For people of color, the answer is simple: "Now and in the future!" The further back you go for communities of color, the worse it gets. Let's not go there.

8. "WE NEED TO RESTORE OUR CHRISTIAN FOUNDATIONS"

Our friend and then-pastor Scott Hagan once sent me (Rick) to Atlanta with our friend Kerry Watts, who is African American. Our assignment was to look at a new children's ministry and see how our church could adapt and apply what was going on. During a short layover in Memphis, a woman who can best be described as a classic Southern belle boarded the plane. She moved quickly to her seat next to Kerry and me and began a dialogue that lasted almost an hour.

Ingratiating, vivacious, attractive, and enigmatic, this woman began the conversation (it would be more accurate to call it a monologue) with her enthusiastic excitement about the upcoming release of *Gods and Generals*, a Civil War movie that she believed would be "free of all that revisionist history those Yankee filmmakers have kept producing for years. At last, someone's going to tell our story!"

She was only too willing to talk about the story of "true Southern heritage." In her view, this heritage was about Christianity, gentility, honor, and civility. To make sure I retained her message, she gave me a series of tracts that extolled the glorious Christian character of Robert E. Lee, Stonewall Jackson, and other heroes of the Confederacy.

The fact that Kerry, an African American—who might have a different view of the story she was spinning—was sitting through her whole presentation never gave her pause. The woman's mythology honeycombed history with gentility, virtue, honor, and civility, and wrapped it all in a pretty Christian bow.

But despite the wrapping, the facts remain: the founders of our nation were slave-owning plantation patriarchs who did not practice orthodox Christianity. Slavery and genocide are not supported in the Bible, and the Constitution is not a sacred document; it never mentions the Bible or the name of Jesus Christ. We'll look at this idea more in chapter 6, but for now we'll reiterate: America is not and has never been a Christian nation.

9. "THIS CONVERSATION MAKES ME UNCOMFORTABLE"

This sentence is often all a white person has to say to excuse herself from a conversation about race. It elevates her own needs above the needs of any people of color in the room. The results are debilitating and reactive. Whatever we had been discussing gets forgotten in the desire to make this white person comfortable and make things easier for her. When we talk this way, we lose sight of two important points: one, if you want change, you have to be willing to be uncomfortable; and two, the feelings of white people do not always need to be placated.

Instead of letting the conversation end or trying to placate the person who feels ill at ease, we would be more productive if we asked a series of questions. Why does this conversation make you uncomfortable? Are you afraid you're losing something? Does this conversation change your identity? How? A person can be transformed when she's willing to truly be transparent and show her ability and vulnerability in the process of change. And that transformation is powerful.

Sometimes we try to assuage our discomfort with easy fixes that telegraph transformation without actually accomplishing it. In my work, I (Skot) have often talked about "event-centered diversity" being the most comfortable and least obtrusive for people in management. It's anchored in what's called the "social imperative"—that is, we're doing this because it's the right thing to do. Event- or moment-centered diversity events are planned by the "mugs and T-shirts" crowd responsible for the quarterly or semiannual "diversity lunch." These gatherings are a feel-good fest with awards, skits, and, at one luncheon we know of, a jar of multicolored "diversa-beans." The trouble is that the message doesn't go very deep or last very long. Most of the time this programmatic approach is short-lived, gone when the bean counters work out the austerity budget.

Take your pick: superficial attempts at diversity that leave people feeling good but unchanged, or multiethnic teams that can solve problems through the transcendent power of difference. The second option is going to be harder. It's going to make most of us uncomfortable at times. But given the rewards, both personally and professionally, isn't discomfort a price worth paying?

10. "IT'S NOT A SKIN PROBLEM; IT'S A SIN PROBLEM"

As Christians, we are very good at making up catchy phrases. These statements can easily distract from the real issues at hand and allow us to avoid dealing with the social issues of our time. We are thus inclined to say things like "We don't have a skin problem; we have a sin problem." Or "It's really all about forgiveness. We just have to forgive the sins of the past." These kinds of statements derail conversation. They are the Christianese version of "Get over it."

Christians agree that we all have to deal with sin, and most of us want to forgive. So if we challenge these statements, we may seem to be going against orthodox teaching. It's hard to find footing when someone harpoons the details with big, theological ideas.

Yet statements like "It's not a skin problem; it's a sin problem" are meant only to avoid the hard truths about the history and legacy of slavery. In order for us to deal with our sin problem and be able to forgive, we have to shine light on our wounds. After all, we are called to be salt and light, and salt and light can only heal when they are placed on the wounded places themselves. True forgiveness and repentance are only possible when we look full-on at the wounds that racism has left in all of us. As our friends at Coming to the Table, an antiracism organization, are fond of saying, "Slavery wounded all of us—black and white—just in different ways." To heal, to forgive, to move on—to get over it—we need to own up to our sin by looking it square in the face.

TOOLS OF TRANSFORMATION

It can be challenging to address these statements when they arise, but address them we must. In our own discomfort, we cannot let these falsehoods and deflections stand. Instead, we need to challenge them by asking gentle but direct questions that force the speaker to think critically about what she or he has said. What makes you say that slaves were treated well? Why do we want to pretend there are no differences in people's skin color? What is the definition of an American?

By asking people to pause, engage, and interrogate their own statements, we can encourage them to see the flaws and harm in their own words, and that sight can lead to healing. When we explore our motivations behind these phrases, and when we gently but clearly challenge their use by others, we can use them as agents of change. Instead of allowing these claims to stop the conversation, we can make them tools of transformation.

DISCUSSION QUESTIONS

- In personal conversations, how often do you hear statements like the ones outlined in this chapter?

- Do you identify with any of these comments? Have you ever said any or thought any of them?

- Can you give an example of one such statement that you heard recently?

- How do you generally respond when you are in conversations about race? What posture do you try to take?

- How difficult is it to confront friends and family members? Why do you think that is?

3

HOW TO KNOW WHAT YOU DON'T KNOW
The Face of Plantation Jesus

W HEN A WHITE FRIEND of ours was about fifteen years old, she learned a term she had never heard before. On the school bus one day, her African American friend Anna said she needed lotion because she was ashy. Our friend looked at her askance and then said she didn't know what *ashy* meant. Anna smiled and said, "My skin is dry. See, it gets gray. It's ashy."

That was the first of many moments in our friend's life when she realized that *she didn't know what she didn't know* about black life and culture. In many ways, it was a minor thing to not know. Yet that experience demonstrates well an important moment in many of our lives: the moment we realize that not only do we not know everything, *we don't even know what we don't know.*

When we created our faith-based diversity curriculum called *Color School*, we established three very different levels of knowledge.

1. *I know what I know.* When we sit down to do the work we are trained to do—be that teaching a third-grade class, replacing an engine block, or setting out a financial plan—we are working from what we know, and we know we do it well. We know what we know.

2. *I know what I don't know.* But if we are placed in circumstances that are new and require us to do things we haven't studied or practiced—ask an auto mechanic to teach high school algebra, for example, or an algebra teacher to diagnose an engine problem—all our comfort and confidence vanish. We suddenly know what we don't know.

3. *I don't know what I don't know.* Sometimes, however, we operate in a way that presumes a level of knowledge we don't have. Take, for instance, a household plumber who believes she can repair a metropolitan water system, or an architect who thinks he understands the soil needs of a rose garden. We assume that what we know about how things work extends to every situation. This third kind of knowledge—not even knowing what we don't know—can be dangerous.

In deeply rooted ignorance and denial, many white Christians take an untenable position when they focus on American racial history. They walk into walls because they lack language, historical context, and cultural sensitivity. This kind of ignorance is not bliss. This kind of silence is not golden.

We are the most unintentionally toxic when we are un-aware of our own ignorance: when we don't know what we don't know. It is this third kind of knowing (or actually *not* knowing) that we examine in this chapter. We'll look at this through the lens of how our Savior is portrayed in theater, art, film, and other forms of popular culture.

THE WHITE BABY IN THE MANGER

For many of us, Christmas is a special time of year. We feel full of goodwill and joy as we celebrate the beautiful birth of a baby who came with the intention of showing us the way to live. That is a glorious thing. Every manger scene, every seasonal play, pageant, and presentation is a treat. We see the baby Jesus—sometimes a doll, sometimes a living infant—and smile.

If we are white, that baby often looks like us, and that feels good. Right. Normal. We don't question it. We do not know what we don't know. We don't understand how damaging Eurocentric imagery is to people of color.

Let's define a term here before moving on. *Eurocentric* means that we place the experience of people of European descent at the center of our personal understanding of cul-ture. Eurocentrism is a particular kind of ethnocentrism. Any form of ethnocentrism centers on "the belief in the inherent superiority of one's own ethnic group or culture."[1] Within this mindset, there is a strong tendency to see any-thing foreign or alien as "other" because of the perspective of one's own cultural norms. In a Eurocentric context, white people unconsciously move in a "master of the universe" grid and place a Western European view of the world as the standard for humanity. European American language, culture, and history constantly define what is true, beautiful, honest, funny, and correct.

All cultures contain elements of structural bias, but Eurocentrism is by far the most powerful and ubiquitous in religious imagery. This type of ethnocentrism comes into sharp focus when we examine our own portrayals of the baby in the manger.

During one Christmas season, I (Rick) received an email from family members whom I deeply love but who did not know what they did not know. They were excited to share a video clip called "Social Network Christmas," which perennially blasts around the Internet, drawing millions of hits. On the surface, a lot of good things appear to be going on in the video: a contemporary way of sharing an old story as a Facebook conversation; putting the gospel in a language and context relevant to new and younger demographics; portraying Bible characters (Joseph, Mary, Elizabeth, and others) as real people living real life. What's not to like?

The moment I saw Joseph's profile picture, however, everything changed. With a complete disregard for evidence, the creators had made all the characters white Europeans. Worst of all, no one seemed to notice—least of all those who enthusiastically passed this material around the web. This anthropological impossibility escaped the millions of viewers of a Facebook Christmas story and the millions of others who have viewed a white Christmas story ever since it became prevalent during the European Renaissance. A white baby Jesus reinforces the Eurocentric idea that whiteness is better. Such "casting" of the human infant who was Jesus as a white child denies the historical facts of Jesus' actual ethnic and cultural heritage, which we look at in the next section. It replaces him with a white child, a child born with the most privilege of any person in the history of the world.

When we cast baby Jesus as a child of European descent even though anthropology, history, and sociology clearly provide evidence to the contrary, we reveal the Eurocentric nature of American Christian religious practice. Plantation Jesus is a white, European god whose son came to earth as a white infant. Venerating Plantation Jesus, even as a baby in the manger, is, quite simply, a form of idolatry.

When white Christians assume that baby Jesus was white just like them, they don't know what they don't know.

THE WHITE SAVIOR

As we look at popular portrayals of Jesus beyond the manger, after he has become a man, it's pretty much the same story. Eurocentric imagery—especially in the depiction of Jesus himself—has repeatedly been expressed in art, pageantry, film, iconography, and church drama. This portrayal of Christ is a toxic element in the global presentation of Christianity.

In 2004, Mel Gibson's film *The Passion of the Christ* was promoted as one of the most accurate depictions of Jesus' last twelve hours. With dialogue in Aramaic and a brutally realistic depiction of the cross, the film moved many viewers deeply. But far from historically accurate are the decidedly European features of actor Jim Caviezel, who played Jesus.

In major films before and since *The Passion*—including *The Greatest Story Ever Told*, *The Robe*, *Jesus of Nazareth*, *The Jesus Film*, *King of Kings*, and *Son of God*—Eurocentric imagery also prevails.

In 2013, the enthusiasm and energy of the Christian community was in high gear with the debut of *The Bible*, a History Channel miniseries. Creators Roma Downey, of *Touched by an Angel*, and Mark Burnett, a producer of *Survivor*, as well as all manner of Christian media, were pleased with record ratings and the fact that nearly seventy million people were "seeing" the Bible. Series supporters lined up quickly; these included Rick Warren, Frank Wright, The Dove Foundation, Phil Cooke, and Life.Church. Downey and Burnett courted the endorsements of "hundreds of Christian leaders," and producers promised that the accuracy of the series was enhanced by "many Christian scholars [who] served as advisors."[2]

However, the series had one very major and sadly predictable flaw. Viewers were not seeing the events of the Bible portrayed by people of color who resembled the historical persons of the time. The actors in the miniseries were, almost exclusively, white people. Jesus was—yet again—played by a European American man. Once again the Eurocentric face of Christianity was perpetuated, the lie of the white Jesus sustained, and the calculated deception of centuries upheld.

"While widely advertising a 'Hispanic' Jesus, the producers actually cast a Portuguese actor . . . with white skin as Jesus," writes Episcopal priest Wil Gafney about the series. "His skin has to be white since Roma Downey . . . cast herself as the Blessed Virgin Mary."[3] Further, when black people were cast in this drama, Gafney writes, their images were used to "reinscribe some of the most base racialized stereotypes in the Americas."[4] In the miniseries, a white actor has his skin darkened for his role as Satan. The devil is brought to the screen in blackface.

We could go on—Russell Crowe as Noah in the film by that name, Christian Bale as Moses in *Exodus*—but the problem is clear. All this "Bible viewing" won't help white Christians own their history or present an accurate view of the biblical narrative. Rather, watching these films allows for and even reinforces racial segregation in churches. The connection is not causal, but it's clear that such racialized biblical media normalizes, for white viewers, sociologist Michael Emerson's finding that "85 percent of congregations in the United States were comprised of at least 90 percent of one group."[5] Rather than actually presenting the truth of the Bible with accurate representations of the human beings involved—a task that surely should not be that hard and that would help Christians begin to question the homogeneous makeup of most of our churches—we choose, instead, to reinforce white supremacy with our casting choices.

White Jesus is the default position, the "factory setting" of Eurocentric Christianity. And white he is, in both large and small church dramas around the United States. At one of our churches in Grand Rapids, two large-scale theater presenta-tions drew thousands each year during Christmas and Easter. These labor-intensive productions took hundreds of volun-teers thousands of hours to produce and maintain. Yet no one involved ever asked how authentic our portrayals of Jesus or his disciples really were. Year after year, the same group of white women and men were asked to play key roles in the story of the Gospels. This was a major failing on our part—a failing that hurt all our members, regardless of their ethnicity.

If we're not accurately portraying the people of that time, we are creating God in our own image. We are making God look like us. That's troubling. For many African American Christians, images of a white Jesus are more than troubling. They completely misrepresent our Christian faith by bringing the worst aspects of plantation dynamics back to life.

So if Jesus wasn't white, what was he?

A MAN OF COLOR

Let's be clear: Jesus was a man of color. He was not European. He was a man from the region of the world that we now call "the Middle East," so he looked far more like people from modern-day Israel-Palestine or Iran than those from Germany or Norway. If we were looking to bring historical accuracy to our nativity stages and tableaus, we would have a dark-skinned woman holding a brown-skinned baby. If we were interested in portraying the truth in our Jesus films and our Easter pageants, we'd have people of color playing all the roles.

In 2002, *Popular Mechanics* published an interesting depiction of Jesus.[6] Using a relatively new scientific method of discovery called forensic anthropology, a team of British scientists and Israeli archaeologists worked to depict what this most famous face in history probably looked like. In the image, Jesus is a man with olive skin; dark, coarse hair; a full beard and moustache; and dark eyes. His jawline is broad and his brow pronounced. In short, he looks like a man from northern Africa or the region we now call the Middle East, and is fairly nondescript in appearance.

This depiction aligns well with Isaiah's prophecy about Jesus' physical appearance: "He had no form or majesty that we should look at him, nothing in his appearance that we should desire him" (Isaiah 53:2). Isaiah's conclusion here that Christ was very ordinary in appearance—a typical Galilean Semite—seems to line up with history and anthropology. Had Jesus looked white and European, he would have been an anomaly in his culture and time. Had he been white, surely his appearance would have been noted in the gospel accounts as either another reason for the religious leadership to persecute him or as a reason for the Roman authorities to protect him as "one of their own."

Additionally, the Bible records King Herod's intention to kill all Hebrew boys under the age of two, so Jesus and his family were instructed to hide in Egypt (Matthew 2:13). It would not be possible for a white, blond-haired, blue-eyed baby to hide among a population of people with dark skin, dark hair, and dark eyes. Furthermore, had Jesus been white, his parents likely wouldn't have had to flee the country, since they could have claimed they were taking care of a Roman family's child.

When Jesus was an adult, after feeding five thousand people with no apparent source of food, he "realized that they were about to come and take him by force to make him king, [and] he withdrew again to the mountain by himself" (John 6:15). Apparently, Jesus could effectively blend into a crowd when necessary, sliding into the general population without notice. When Judas was setting up his betrayal of Christ, he had to prearrange a signal with the Roman soldiers—"The one I will kiss is the man; arrest him" (Matthew 26:48). If Jesus had been white, Judas wouldn't have needed to single him out in such a way.

Thus, nothing about the biblical account gives any indication that Jesus was anything but a man who looked like the citizens of his birth community in the area we now call the Middle East. "The fact that he probably looked a great deal more like a darker-skinned Semite than westerners are used to seeing him pictured is a reminder of his universality," said Charles Hackett of Emory University's Candler School of Theology. "And [it is] a reminder of our tendency to appropriate him in the service of our cultural values."[7]

Once we understand how these images reinforce the belief systems that undergirded the practice of plantation slavery, we begin to see the profound depth of this problem. A few years ago, when I (Rick) challenged the authenticity and historical accuracy of these images in a newspaper article about the paintings of Warner Sallman,[8] the artist who painted the most ubiquitous image of Jesus as a blond-haired, blue-eyed man in *Head of Christ*, I received an angry call from an elderly woman.

"Young man," she said, "I'll have you know that picture has been in the narthex of our church for the last forty years." I found it an interesting way to argue for the rightness of that portrayal. It was as if the longevity of the error made it acceptable.

The claim to tradition is not hers alone. But tradition does not support accuracy. We can be sincere, but we can also be sincerely wrong.

DOES IT MATTER?

When anyone brings this obvious conundrum—white depictions of Jesus when all evidence points to the contrary—to the level of reasonable inquiry in churches around the country, the typical response is "It really doesn't matter." Warner Sallman's Jesus in the church lobby? No big deal. Pageants and movies and artwork that get it wrong? They're just details. The children's storybook with a white baby in the manger? It doesn't really matter in the bigger scheme of things. Right?

Historian Rik Stevenson, a frequent guest on our radio show, once said, "It really doesn't matter—as long as Jesus is white." Indeed, how we portray Jesus—the image that many believe "does not matter"—*does* matter, for several reasons. When we represent our Savior as a European American man, the message we send is devastating.

First, when our children are surrounded by images of a white Jesus, they formulate a clear portrait in their minds of what God looks like. At a conference in Grand Rapids, author Tim Wise shared a conversation between his two daughters about the film *Evan Almighty*. In the film, the protagonist Evan, played by Steve Carell, is told by God that a flood is imminent and that he should make an ark and line up animals two by two. God is played by African American actor Morgan Freeman. When Wise's four-year-old daughter asked if Freeman was God, his six-year-old daughter piped up, "That can't be God, because God isn't black. God is white."[9]

As Wise said during his conference talk, "That showed me how normal and how toxic this imagery is. As a parent, I can control the books, movies, and resource materials that come into my house. But when this kind of poison is literally in the air everywhere and never critically examined, the challenge to maintain an antiracist perspective is profoundly difficult."

Second, white images of Jesus provide a mask that legitimizes and covers for slavery, Reconstruction, Jim Crow, and the mass incarceration of people of color. Appropriating Jesus as white is the first step in accepting more extreme horrors as God's will. Under Plantation Jesus' white visage, oppression and bias—as well as rape, kidnapping, torture, murder, and current systemic disparities—can all come to be seen as the "divine order of things," as theologian James Cone notes in his book *The Cross and the Lynching Tree*.[10]

In his article "Children of a White God: A Study of Racist 'Christian' Theologies," theologian Matthew Ogilvie reveals a common thread among white separatists, supremacists, nationalists, anti-Semites, and nativists: the belief that Jesus was white. If so many people who believe that white people are innately superior to people of color hold as one of their central tenets that Jesus was white, we must acknowledge that this white rewriting of Jesus' historical identity is deeply connected to racism.[11]

Further, when churches display prominent white members of the community—the local founding fathers, the "good people" of the region—on plaques and pictures placed near stained glass icons and paintings of a white European Jesus, the net effect is to support white supremacy and race-based bias. Although these well-meaning and sincere folks don't know what they don't know, the undeniable message—contained in "artwork, still pictures, manger scenes, magazines, religious study material and heroes in plays," writes Michael Emerson in *People of the Dream*—is a monocultural covering put in place by dominant groups.[12]

With even the slightest level of awareness and attention, we can identify the subliminal message behind the imagery in churches: God looks white and acts white. White people are the closest thing there is to God on the planet. Therefore, God has placed white people in this favored, dominant position.

A person of color, then, has two choices with regard to mostly white churches or denominations, or with churches that have not come to terms with racist imagery and language. She can assimilate, or she can leave. If she stays, even when she is fully acculturated into the "rightness of whiteness," as the late activist Abraham Citron described it, she will always be viewed as "other," a permanent alien and outsider.[13] When Jesus is white, we communicate to people of color that they are welcome . . . as long as they allow themselves to be shaped into a white image. When the face of a white Jesus hangs in a church—defying all we know of what his appearance would have been in the time and place in which he lived—we are telling people of color, "You are welcome, but you will never belong. You must assimilate to the expectations—the white expectations—of this space or always be an outsider. You must choose to be 'like us' if you want to be fully accepted here."

Nothing about this message speaks of the radical love of God. Nothing about the white face of Plantation Jesus reflects the real Christ, who looked less like those in power and more like those who were oppressed.

WHY THE MYTH-MAKING CONTINUES

We have gotten this wrong for so very long that we don't even ask the key question at hand: Why do we need to make Jesus white? The answer to this question is buried by layers of denials that are founded not on facts but on what many white people want desperately to believe. We need Jesus to be white because we are still allegiant to Plantation Jesus and to the racial hierarchy that puts white people on top.

And when we say that we've gotten this wrong for a long time, we mean it. "The calculated distortion of religious imagery began in Europe during the Renaissance," notes writer Miles Willis, adding that this imagery "is still one of the most effective and enduring tools of white supremacy."[14] In nineteenth-century America, Eurocentric imagery of all sorts became imprinted into the public consciousness. It was during this time in our history that we were defining citizenship, growing the economy, and pushing Native Americans to the west, note Edward Blum and Paul Harvey, authors of *The Color of Christ*.[15] At just the moment when America was defining what it really meant to be an American, we assigned privilege to the white identity, placing all other people in positions of lesser access and opportunity, at best, and outright oppression at worst.

Within this framework of racial superiority, it became acceptable to own other human beings as long as they were black, and to force Native Americans off their land because white people had a right to claim the land. Without the crimes of Eurocentric imagery, it would be much easier to expose this injustice and oppression, but within it, anything—no matter how heinous—is possible. That's why the myth-making continues. It's very hard to know what you don't know when you are living within this system.

Through the corridors of racial history—from Selma to Soweto, from Cape Town to Birmingham, from apartheid to the civil rights movement, from slavery to Jim Crow—the central tenet has always been a Eurocentric, race-based caste system. This system, while it takes different forms, never really has to change, no matter how traumatized, diminished, marginalized, and ignored communities of color feel. White imagery, especially of Jesus, is the face of this system, and it constantly reinforces this most toxic and dangerous part of "normal."

Warner Sallman's Jesus, that beatific image that the elderly woman found so precious, is simply the face of Plantation Jesus: white, fair-haired, thin-faced. He is the unchallenged mainstream image, and the symbol of Eurocentric Christianity. The spirit of this image makes slave history come to life. It communicates to people of color that this religious symbol and the system behind it do not welcome them. This kind of imagery in all its forms must be removed from our congregations' walls, windows, presentations, and pageants.

Indeed, the pervasive mythology of Plantation Jesus is buried within several facts we have to face: Jesus was not white. Eurocentric Christianity is not the global standard. Making God into our image does incredible damage to our Christian witness.

By seeing the face of Plantation Jesus and confronting it, we can finally learn to know what we do not know. And we can begin to take responsibility for it. Only then can we project a consistently inclusive message to everyone, a message that speaks the truth of God's kingdom.

DISCUSSION QUESTIONS

- What kinds of pictures hang on the walls of your home? On the walls at your church?

- What is the message people receive from your congregation's artwork or stained glass? Have you asked them?

- What imagery do you need to change? How could you change it?

- Do people of color have a voice in deciding how things look at your church? If not, why not?

4

WHAT TO BELIEVE
Reading the Bible on the Plantation

FROM SOUTH AFRICA'S South Bantu languages comes the word *ubuntu*. Although we have no
direct translation into English, the basic meaning of *ubuntu*
is clear: it means, in essence, "my humanity is directly connected to yours." *Ubuntu* is the "very essence of being human," says Archbishop Desmond Tutu. "A person is a person
through other persons."[1] We are interconnected. The pains
that hurt one of us hurt all of us. The joys that lift one of us
lift us all.

It is with *ubuntu* in mind that we must enter into our conversations about racism within our faith traditions. *Ubuntu*,
or acknowledging that my humanity is tied up with yours,

is also a good starting point as we begin our conversations about how the Bible has been used to justify and support not only slavery but also white supremacy, racial segregation, and the criminalization of interracial marriage. Remembering our interconnectedness as children of God can help us approach the truths of our history and the facts of our present with grace and compassion, both for ourselves and for others.

This discussion can be hard for some. It is not easy to reflect on the ways that our Scripture—the Bible we know and love—has been used for such malevolent purposes. The Bible can be a mighty sword for good when it is read fully and with the love of God paramount. But it can become a tool of hate when used for our own wills and desires. To help our churches reflect more of what God's kingdom is truly like, we must confront the hard truth about how our holy Bible has been employed for such unholy work. This is the work before us in this chapter.

FAITHFUL OR RECKLESS READING

Any theological and biblical justification of slavery—of which there have historically been many forms—calls forth deeply rooted questions about our humanity. Any justifications for slavery drawn from the Bible are based primarily on our own preexisting cultural conditioning. It is very easy to read Scripture through our own personal, cultural, ethnic, and national perspectives, but that is a work of misinterpretation. When this misinterpretation happens, we as Christians must begin a personal and spiritual journey to correct it. This journey involves the deconstruction of the systems and institutions in which we are still involved that cause harm to other human beings. One of those systems is the very method by which we interpret the Bible.

The method of biblical interpretation most commonly used by the pastors we know is *exegesis*: a critical analysis of Scripture. In its purest and best form, exegesis considers many important factors, including how the passage lines up with the words of Jesus; the original audience to whom the text is addressed; the historical and cultural context of the time period in which the passage is found; and other biblical references on the same topic. No one comes to Scripture with a completely blank page or totally free of cultural and historical bias. But Christians committed to good exegesis will, with time, be able to comprehend the truth and correctly understand what the Bible says, as well as what the Bible does not say.

For example, consider the verses in Leviticus that require an Israelite woman to be removed from the company of men and the house of God during her menstrual cycle (see, for example, Leviticus 15). Good exegetical study of those verses shows us the cultural understanding of menstruation at that time: that it made a woman unclean, that her uncleanliness was contagious, and that a menstruating woman would transmit her uncleanliness to crops or others she touched during this period of the month. Some scholars believe this separation was ordered for the safety of women, who could be punished for the problems they supposedly caused. Good exegesis of these sections of Leviticus also considers how profoundly Jesus upended these requirements: the story of Jesus' compassionate healing of the woman who was suffering from hemorrhages who touched his cloak (Luke 8:43-48), for example, and his treatment of women throughout this ministry. Thus, exegesis reveals that this provision dealt with the cultural understandings of that historical moment and was not a directive from God that extends to all women at all times in history. Today, we do not require women to be separated from men or from the church building during menstruation.

We do not always practice such sound exegesis, however, especially when it comes to interpreting Scripture from within our deeply rooted patterns of ethnocentrism. When we interpret the Bible without acknowledging our biases, we see Scripture rising to meet and agree with the grid through which we see our faith and the world. If our cultural assumptions are where things begin and end—if we do not attempt to see our own biases—we then read Scripture to meet our own preconceived beliefs. We shape the text instead of allowing the text to shape us.

In other words, when we perform poor exegesis, we read Scripture to support our own worldview. This way of reading means we look for verses of the Bible that appear to justify what we call "the divine order of things"—that is, the way *we* believe things are created. This faulty way of reading Scripture is called *eisegesis*. In eisegesis, we take verses out of context, cut them away from their original meaning, and read them through our own agendas. When we are looking to back up our own biases and prejudices and neglect to read Scripture as a whole, we can easily find "support" for our own beliefs.

Careful and faithful exegesis interprets the text in light of other passages and its original context and audience, as well as in conversation with church tradition and Christian community. Reckless biblical interpretation—eisegesis—imports the reader's own agenda into the Bible and cuts off the particular passage's continuity with history, culture, audience, and the rest of Scripture.

WHAT CAN HAPPEN WHEN WE WARP SCRIPTURE

Once we begin the process of eisegesis, anything is possible. For example, the nefarious but very typical activities related to slavery in the United States—kidnapping, rape, torture, and murder—were justified and "proven" using the Bible by employing verses like Ephesians 6:5 and 1 Peter 2:18. Both passages appear, to some readers, to support slavery by calling slaves to serve their masters.[2]

We know now that these verses speak to a particular cultural and historical moment. We know that our understanding of the larger view of God's love for humanity, read through the lens of the full arc of Scripture and the life of Jesus, makes the enslavement of other human beings a sinful, ungodly act. Yet many white Christians still justify their own racist beliefs with these fragments of Scripture. When we take these verses out of their cultural context and out of the larger context of the nature of God, the theology of oppression is created and sustained. In that way, a faulty manner of reading Scripture becomes an insidious part of everyday life and provides a moral and spiritual covering for crimes against humanity.

It was this work of misinterpretation that justified the actions of Christians who participated in the institution of slavery. But it wasn't just the act of owning human beings that white Christians were permitting when they warped Scripture in this way. White Christians used the Bible to justify even further horrors against enslaved people, covering their sins with a whitewashing of biblical language. Take, for instance, the evangelizing of enslaved people. While some argue that Christianity was shared with enslaved Africans because of a desire to save their souls, the facts of the matter were much more sinister. "Christianity was not presented to black people in America to enlighten and empower them," historian Rik Stevenson said on our radio show one day; rather, Christianity was presented to slaves "to subjugate and oppress them."

Many enslaved people *did* adopt and shape Christianity, infusing their newfound faith with personal and communal experiences of their own. Yet while those traditions remain life-changing for many African Americans and those of us blessed to be a part of communities where these traditions thrive, the fact remains: Christian faith was used as a weapon to shackle enslaved people. By requiring enslaved people to take on the mantle of Christianity, slave masters further erased the traditional religions and customs of their native lands and tribal origins. A people separated from their faith are much easier to control. Evangelizing their slaves gave white Christians a "reason" for enslavement that went beyond, in their minds, selfish greed. Now they could claim that these dark-skinned people were being saved for all eternity. Subjugation becomes salvation.

This subjugation was accomplished in part by misrepresenting, misinterpreting, and purposefully mistranslating the word *slave* in the New Testament. The most accurate meaning of the word *doulos*—translated repeatedly from the New Testament Greek as "slave"—is actually "bond servant." Indentured or bond service was a method of paying off debts that had a legally defined beginning and end. For most of history, including the period in which the Bible was written, "indentured servant" would be a common understanding of the word *doulos*. In fact, in the Old Testament, under the theocratic rule of Israel's kings, people with debts would work them off as indentured servants. But in the year of Jubilee—which occurred every fifty years—all debts were canceled, as delineated in Leviticus 25. Thus even indentured servants were freed.

Indentured servitude was also a common type of labor in the early seventeenth-century American colonies and in many cultures, including African cultures, around the world. Thus, connections to indentured servants or bond servants would have resonated within both Old Testament and New Testament cultures and the colonial culture of North America and Europe. But the unusually cruel and uniquely American system—in which enslavement passed from mother to child and where kidnapping, rape, torture, and murder were part and parcel of the practice that evolved into the race-based, transatlantic slave trade—would not. Slavery is in the Bible, but Scripture does not support chattel slavery (ownership of humans) by race or for any other reason. The use of the word *slave* as the translation of *doulos* in these passages is inaccurate and was primarily driven by white supremacy in order to advance the economic interests of white slaveholders.

Plantation Jesus is at work here as well in our historical and contemporary readings of Scripture. This false god's systems made it possible for people to misinterpret Scripture, allowing their own cultural biases to shape how they read the Bible so that they could use it for their own purposes. Thus, black people were "spiritually" perceived as being "cursed by God" because Noah's son Ham (believed by legend to be the ancestor of all black people) saw his father naked (Genesis 9:20-27). By isolating this passage and connecting it to an impossible and unsupported leap of faith, white people could reach the conclusion that blacks were cursed forever to serve white people. Thus, the racist belief in the "curse of Ham" developed. (Also, for the record, in that passage God actually cursed Ham's son Canaan.)

Or take the passage that Southern Baptists once used to justify slavery and segregation. Southern Baptists used to think that the "mark of Cain" mentioned in Genesis 4:11-16 was a "curse of black skin," which Cain received from God for the murder of his brother, Abel. Using this same misinterpretation, the Church of Jesus Christ of Latter-day Saints kept African Americans out of pulpits until 1978.

Nowhere is eisegesis more obvious than in antebellum slave catechisms that were commonly taught to captive populations in the mid–nineteenth century. In these texts, Christianity is presented as a form of indoctrination and control ordained by God and centered on slave masters and mistresses who are, in the false hierarchy of human worth, valued as coming just below their Creator.

Q. Who gave you your master and your mistress?

A. *God gave them to me.*

"Slaves, obey your earthly masters with respect and fear, and with sincerity of heart, just as you would obey Christ" (Ephesians 6:5, *NIV*).

Q. Who says you must obey them?

A. *God says I must.*

"Slaves, obey your earthly masters in everything, not only while being watched and in order to please them, but wholeheartedly, fearing the Lord" (Colossians 3:22). "Tell slaves to be submissive to their masters and to give satisfaction in every respect; they are not to talk back . . ." (Titus 2:9).

Q. What book tells you these things?

A. *The Bible.*[3]

Obviously, the Bible does not tell us the things these catechisms purported. Scripture does not justify, approve, or endorse slavery based on white supremacy. Black people are not cursed by God to serve white people in a fixed, perpetual, immutable hierarchy. And the codified segregation and state-sponsored terrorism of Jim Crow—a fixture of the Bible Belt in the southern United States until relatively recently—is not supported by any pastor or theologian who really knows what the Bible says and does not say.

READING THROUGH THE JESUS LENS

So how can we know whether we are reading the Bible faithfully or whether we are using it to serve our own agendas? How can we make sure we are applying it to our lives in a way that reflects the true nature of God and God's kingdom? One principle of faithful exegesis is reading the Bible through the lens of Jesus' life, teachings, death, and resurrection. Jesus said, toward the end of his ministry, "All authority in heaven and on earth has been given to me" (Matthew 28:18). Pastor Palmer Becker writes, "While we give authority to all Scriptures, we interpret and obey them through the words, spirit, and nature of Jesus."[4] The teachings of Jesus—as seen in his interaction with the Canaanite woman and his parable of the good Samaritan, to choose just two examples—make it clear that our role as Christians is to show compassion and love to all people. Jesus modeled for us a way of being that completely flattened hierarchies of personal worth.

In addition to reading the Bible in light of Jesus Christ, we must read passages of Scripture in light of other parts of the Bible. Again, pulling passages out of historical context and the larger framework of the arc of Scripture as a whole distorts the Word of God and makes it serve our own purposes instead of the purposes of the kingdom. For example, historian Susan Wise Bauer points to New Testament passages like "Slaves, obey your masters" as descriptive statements within the historical, cultural context of first-century experience. But supporters of American slavery used these passages as prescriptive commands to endorse their belief that slavery was right and justified. To perpetuate this harm, they had to ignore "all of the minor prophets and everything that was said in the Old Testament about social justice." Bauer notes that it was "a selective literalism, which we still see in Christianity today."[5]

Another critical principle in biblical interpretation is recognizing that equality, not hierarchy or subjugation, is the norm in kingdom relationships. Paul writes to the Galatian church, "There is no longer Jew or Greek, there is no longer slave or free, there is no longer male and female; for all of you are one in Christ Jesus" (Galatians 3:28). In the book of Philemon, when the apostle Paul confronts the owner-slave relationship spiritually and socioeconomically, his conclusions are very clear. In his conversion experience, Onesimus, a former slave, now has a different relationship with Philemon, his former master. As one commentator says, "Philemon is to regard Onesimus as an equal, his Christian 'brother' (v. 16) and 'partner' in the faith (v. 17), which makes their owner-slave relationship no longer possible. So Paul is sending Onesimus back to Philemon for their reconciliation; they are *both* his spiritual sons, and he is the religious patron and responsible for the nurture of both."[6]

Plantation Jesus has created a theology of oppression, a God-approved hierarchy with white European Americans on top and everyone else oppressed below. But the real Jesus frees us from oppression and sin and ushers in a kingdom in which all dwell together as sisters and brothers in Christ. Plantation Jesus' system reinforces "the political and social doctrine of white supremacy, the belief that whites are innately superior to and possess the right of hegemony over dark-skinned people."[7] But the real Jesus' system is built on restoration, justice, reconciliation, and the beloved community.

STILL READING ON THE PLANTATION

Lest we think that Plantation Jesus' chokehold on biblical interpretation is a thing of the past, we must look at contemporary manifestations of racially unjust eisegesis. In so many ways, both mundane and startling, the Christian church still operates in this same way.

In July 2012, a pastors' conference open to "All White Christians" was held near Winfield, Alabama, and hosted by Rev. William J. Collier's Church of God's Chosen. "We're bringing the Word of God to people who want it," a conference organizer said, clarifying that they believe white people are "part of the chosen race."[8] In video footage of the event, KKK banners and white supremacy flags are on display. Many residents of the small western Alabama town were upset, and the business community was outraged. "The city of Winfield does not condone this," said Winfield's mayor.[9]

Yet, as is typical when events of racial injustice occur, most of the predominately white evangelical churches in the area were deafeningly silent. Had you asked them directly, most churchgoers would have certainly condemned the bigotry of this racist group. But by simply being silent, white evangelicals actually stand in support of Collier's supremacist ideology. White Christians often collude with racist theologies in the conspiracy of their silence, as psychologist and former Spelman College president Beverly Daniel Tatum has written.

We could easily dismiss Collier's gathering as the cartoon-ish stupidity of a lunatic fringe, the Christian Identity movement. Of course white people are not the "chosen race," a status only conferred historically upon Old Testament Israel (Deuteronomy 7:7). Of course Collier and those of his ilk are wrong, "for God shows no partiality" (Romans 2:11). But white supremacy is still surprisingly part of the mainstream, a fact that's evidenced by the vast silence that surrounds even these overt acts of racism in our midst.

White supremacy retains its power when so many white people find fault with counterprotestors in places like Charlottesville or with rioters in places like Baltimore rather than actually engaging with the racism that enflamed the situation in the first place. White supremacy retains power in the silence of white Christians who allow their Scriptures to be twisted and tangled to justify racism without feeling the urgency to speak out except to criticize the actions of those who stand on the side of the oppressed.

If we know Jesus Christ—if we understand his heart, if he lives inside us, and if we see the inclusive nature of his king-dom—and if we understand the pervasive brutality and pure evil of the slave trade and the Jim Crow system, we know that we can't be slaveholders. We know we can't be slave traders or KKK members or White Citizens' Council members. That much is clear. But now we must learn that we also can't stand silent when black and brown people are shot to death while seated in their cars. We cannot be silent when Nazis march through a college campus with torches, or when people use our Scriptures to justify racial injustice.

The Jesus of the Bible calls us not to silence but to compassion, hope, and allegiance to God's kingdom. Jesus calls us to love.

DISCUSSION QUESTIONS

- Do you think the Bible is still being used to justify bias and oppression? If so, in what way?

- How can we know that we are interpreting Scripture correctly?

- What can we do when we see our faith being misrepresented?

- How much bad doctrine comes from faulty biblical interpretation? What other examples, in addition to those listed in the chapter, can you offer?

- How do you explain how Bible-based Christianity and race-based chattel slavery coexisted for so long?

5

WHO'S GOT THE POWER?
White Supremacy Doesn't Just
Wear Hoods

O N AUGUST 12, 2017, James Alex Fields Jr.
drove his gleaming Dodge Challenger into a crowd of
people in Charlottesville, Virginia, killing thirty-two-year-old
Heather Heyer and seriously injuring nineteen other people.
That day, Fields and several hundred other white supremacists had marched through the streets of this small city under
the leadership of two clean-cut men who have never donned
a white hood in their lives.

By all appearances, Richard Spencer and Jason Kessler,
two of the most prominent, self-declared white supremacists
in the United States, could have just as easily been deacons
collecting offering on Sunday morning. White supremacy

isn't simply hoods and burning crosses. Just as Spencer and Kessler can espouse their ideas without cover of night or hooded costume, white supremacy doesn't just fester among fringe groups or in the beliefs of racist radicals. White supremacy is part and parcel of American culture. The terms *white supremacy* and *white privilege* are often nonstarters in cross-racial conversations. They often provoke denial and pushback from white people, as they did for me (Rick) when Skot first brought these words into our dialogue. I couldn't imagine how either of these terms had anything to do with me. After all, I was loving to everyone I met, regardless of race, and I certainly wasn't a member of a hate group.

Many white people assume that white privilege is something possessed only by America's bluebloods—WASPs with Ivy League degrees and relatives on the Mayflower. Many think white supremacy is all about extreme racial hate groups, like the cross-burning Klansmen of the American South or the Aryan Nation or the Christian Identity movement. But if we dig deeper, we learn that privilege and supremacy are written into the very structure of life in the United States.

White people do not ask to benefit from white privilege or white supremacy, and we may not even want these benefits. But they are ours nonetheless. Denial and silence about this privilege and supremacy will not make them go away. Ignorance about them is not bliss. The only way we will shed the unearned benefits of our white skin is to dismantle privilege and disrupt the systems of white supremacy so that all people are given the same opportunities, benefits, and treatment.

But before we can begin to dismantle systems, we must understand them. Let's make sure we understand what we mean when we talk about white privilege and white supremacy. Then we will look at some of the ways privilege and supremacy function to redefine who the founding fathers were and what type of society we live in.

DEFINING THE TERMS

White privilege, according to the field of study known as critical race theory, is a set of advantages enjoyed by white people that are unavailable to nonwhite people in the same social, political, and economic spaces.[1] People who benefit from white privilege are not necessarily aware of it, and therefore do not see themselves as racist or prejudiced. Privilege is a salient characteristic of every white European living in the United States, past and present. If we are born with white skin in America, we are born with the benefits of white privilege, whether we like it or not.

Having white privilege doesn't preclude being underprivileged in other areas, as many people believe. For example, a person can have white privilege and still be poor or undereducated, just as a person can be black and have economic privilege. Privilege in one area does not guarantee privilege in all areas.

In her essay "White Privilege: Unpacking the Invisible Knapsack," scholar Peggy McIntosh says, "I have come to see white privilege as an invisible package of unearned assets that I can count on cashing in each day, but about which I was 'meant' to remain oblivious." She lists several of the ways that white European Americans experience privilege, including "I can be sure that my children will be given curricular materials that testify to the existence of their race" and "I am never asked to speak for all the people of my racial group."[2] Privilege is insidious and powerful, but unlike more obvious results of racism in our country, such as hate crimes or racial slurs, it is subtle and hard to detect unless we choose to identify it. Thus if we want to break down the systems that oppress people of color, we need to recognize privilege and eliminate it through work to create a truly "equal playing field" for everyone. If we benefit from privilege, we are responsible for it.

White privilege is a deception. It's idolatrous. It's a handshake with the devil throughout history. It's complicit with evil, and it's not something that a person of color should long for.

White supremacy, then, is the *system* behind the privilege: the system that operates on the foundational belief that white people are superior to people of all other racial groups and ethnicities. Antiracist educator Tim Wise calls it "the operationalized form of racism in the United States and throughout the Western world."[3] While white supremacy is often connected to hate groups like the Ku Klux Klan and the White Citizens' Councils, it is in fact simply the system in which we in the United States operate, a system that privileges white people above any other group. White supremacy is carved into the foundation of our country's history and structure. White people are advantaged by systems of white supremacy, whether they like it or not.

Often, white people are shocked and outraged when they learn the extent to which white supremacy is still operative in America. White people still curry unmerited favor in the world of white supremacy. This is one of those things, as we discussed in chapter 3, that many white people don't know that they don't know. Many white people are ignorant of such historical practices as real estate "redlining," a practice that kept people of color out of certain neighborhoods and that increased residential segregation. Many are surprised when they learn of the racial disparities evidenced in our systems of mass incarceration, where 38 percent of all people imprisoned are black, in comparison to the overall general population where 13 percent are black.[4] Or consider that the median white household now has a net wealth thirteen times greater than that of the median black household.[5] These are just some of the many instances where white privilege is easily apparent.

White privilege and supremacy work by giving some people an advantage, a head start in life. Corporate diversity trainer Ron Jimmerson, a dear friend of ours, tells a story to illustrate how privilege and supremacy work. Imagine a baseball game between two very competitive teams: Team A and Team B. Team B has rolled up a huge score, 20–0, when it's discovered that they've been cheating. "Okay," Team B says, "we'll start playing by the rules now. But the score is still 20–0." Imagine how frustrating it would be to compete in a game you love, only to face insurmountable deficits based on inequity you can't remedy. People of color face this kind of unjust score daily.

True Christian faith stands against this type of injustice. A perspective on human worth that puts Christ at the center demands change from everybody. Thus, we do not deny the existence of this demonic, invisible system of privilege and power. We do, however, deny it the right to rule over us or to determine our level of success or our destiny. Only God has the final say on that. White people are not the source of change; rather, we focus on Christ. It is Christ who can bring about change.

Followers of Jesus are called to operate out of *covenant* privilege, not white privilege. We sometimes call it kingdom privilege: the gift of belonging to the kingdom of God that is available to all. Covenant privilege is not complicit with evil, and it does not benefit from another's suffering. Kingdom privilege is the true freedom and gift of living in Christ, rather than the warped benefits that accrue in an ethnic or race-based merit system. We know that the Spirit of God is stronger than the spirit of racism. Thus, people of color don't look to white people to change by acknowledging their privilege—if you want to call this deceptive form of idolatry *privilege*—and subsequently battling against white supremacy. Rather, as followers of Christ, we situate ourselves within the work of God, because we know that God is all powerful. We know that God's kingdom is a place of equality and value for all people, where only God is supreme.

THOMAS JEFFERSON: HERO OR ANTIHERO?

Many of us want to claim that America is a privilege-free meritocracy that somehow echoes heaven by operating on the words of Founding Father Thomas Jefferson: a place where "all men are created equal."

But America is not a meritocracy where everyone gets exactly what they earn regardless of their race, ethnicity, gender, or economic class. America is built on a systemic hierarchy that privileges white, male, straight, wealthy people and oppresses people who do not fit into all or even one of these categories. If we look honestly at Jefferson's life, we begin to see that his language in the Declaration of Independence is merely rhetoric, not something built on an idea of true equality at all.

In fact, no one in American history is more responsible for the well-established pattern of white supremacy and privilege than Thomas Jefferson. Far from being the Saint Thomas of the religious right or Professor Jefferson, the celebrated thinker and Renaissance man of the political left, the master of Monticello was actually a "coldblooded taskmaster who ruthlessly exploited child labor and overworked his slaves as a matter of course."[6] Henry Wiencek's book *Master of the Mountain* provides, at long last, a view of Jefferson as a slave owner and master of Virginia's premier plantation, who lived like a pharaoh and made enormous profits from "the peculiar institution" of slavery.[7]

As Wiencek said on our radio show in 2012, "Many of these facts about Jefferson's relationship to slavery as an institution and his slaves in particular have been known for a long time. It's just that we've covered them in honey and not really unpacked what the extensive records at Monticello reveal." That's far from the only thing about Jefferson's life that is covered in honey. In the sweet-sounding prose of *Notes on the State of Virginia*, Jefferson talks openly about his "deep personal distaste for blacks, who, he asserted, smelled wrong, copulated with apes in Africa, and were incapable of intellectual achievement."[8] Thomas Jefferson was a very human, very broken, very racist man.

So it is a strange turn of events that has many evangelical Christians holding up Jefferson as a one-dimensional good man, and even as a Christian who believed in equality. Several years ago we were leading a program at a church in Holland, Michigan. One evening, we began a session that focused in part on the founding fathers, specifically Thomas Jefferson. We started with facts historians know very well: (a) the number of slaves Jefferson owned throughout his life, including during the years he served as president; (b) the unlikelihood that his relationship with Sally Hemings could be considered "romantic" (as opposed to abusive) within the dynamics of chattel slavery; (c) his deistic beliefs that were well outside of orthodox Christianity, evidenced in part by the infamous "bible" he produced, which omits all references to the Holy Spirit, miracles, and the virgin birth.

When we begin to discuss American racial history, we always expect pushback. But on this particular night, things got especially heated with one white man and his son. "You can't do that," the father told us, "because when one of the founders goes down, they all do. That's just not right; it's not what I've been taught." As his son began to defend his father's position, it became clear to us that the conversation needed to be defused and refocused.

"Could Thomas Jefferson be a member of your church?" I (Rick) asked. "Could he be a deacon or an elder? Could he run your children's program?"

A college student raised his hand. "I did a research paper on Jefferson in school last year," he said. "He couldn't be in leadership here at church. He wouldn't even be able to accept our statement of faith." This student was right. It's hard to imagine Thomas Jefferson being a part of any congregation in America that adheres to orthodox Christianity.

But these facts have not stopped faux historians from crafting the narrative that Jefferson was an upstanding and even evangelical Christian. David Barton—the pied piper of Christian fundamentalism's God-and-country myth machine—and several others are determined to reshape the founders into their own theological and political image. Barton is a frequent guest speaker in large, high-profile, conservative churches all over the country and a trusted advisor to politicians Michele Bachmann, Mike Huckabee, and Newt Gingrich, as well as a supporter of Donald Trump.

Always depicting Christianity as under attack by secularists, Barton cherry-picks his way through the words of the founders to celebrate their faith. Because most pastors aren't trained in historical scholarship and congregations don't fact-check Barton's claims, and because he doesn't open himself to questions during his rapid-fire presentations, Barton is able to present distortions and half-truths that rarely get challenged. In his book *The Jefferson Lies*, Barton claims to expose the myths you've always believed about Jefferson. According to Barton, it is a myth that Jefferson (a) wrote his own version of the Bible, (b) was a racist who opposed civil rights, and (c) advocated the secularization of public life.[9] Barton's goal is to convince readers that Jefferson was an orthodox Christian in every way.

The many credentialed historians who have appeared on our radio show agree that these are not myths, as Barton contends, but rather facts about our third president's life. Thomas Jefferson owned six hundred slaves during his lifetime, including during the years of his presidency. The Bible Jefferson edited *is* devoid of miracles, the Trinity, and the virgin birth; thus, it would not be accepted as true anywhere in evangelical Christian circles. When Jefferson wrote the words "all men are created equal," he clearly did *not* consider African Americans as people God had created equally. Is this racism? Yes. Is this Christianity? No.

After ongoing challenges from historians across the country and the threat of a boycott from a group of pastors in Cincinnati, Barton's publisher, Thomas Nelson, finally decided to fact-check his work.[10] "As we got into it, our conclusion was the criticisms were correct," said Thomas Nelson vice president and publisher Brian Hampton. "There were historical details— matters of fact, not matters of opinion, that were not supported at all."[11] In the summer of 2012, Thomas Nelson pulled *The Jefferson Lies* from store shelves and canceled Barton's contract. But it should make us all uneasy that a Christian publisher allowed the publication of this book and the egregious errors that are a fundamental part of its argument.

When Barton's lies about Jefferson were exposed, we hoped that the faith community would begin to see the

difference between fact and opinion and respond accord-
ingly. Sadly, that didn't happen. Barton has defended himself;
he continues to have a regularly scheduled TV program on
two major Christian television stations, he hosts a daily radio show that airs on almost three hundred stations, and he
purports to speak at churches across the country over four
hundred times a year.[12] As of this writing, his organization
WallBuilders has over 175,000 fans on Facebook, and he has
over 30,000 followers on Twitter. Clearly, the wave of support
for Barton has not ebbed.

THE MYTH OF MERITOCRACY

Barton and his teachings are just one example of a much
larger problem: the cycle of an all-American myth machine
in which white supremacy and privilege remain in the default
position of power. As long as we believe that every person in
the United States has the same opportunities and the same
ability to achieve success, we find it difficult to accept that the
founders of our nation not only believed in white supremacy
but operated within and benefited from systems that intentionally oppressed African Americans and other people of
color. If it's not broke, why fix it? That's what we believe. In reality, while the equality implied in the statement "all men are
created equal" is foundational to the American democratic
ideal, this equality has never actually been lived out.

In presentations for our faith-based diversity curriculum called *Color School*, we would often put John Trumbull's
well-known painting of the signing of the Declaration of
Independence on the screen. Then we'd ask people an easy

question: "As you look at this painting, how many women, people of color, and children do you see?"

The participants would quickly note that there are no people of color or women or children in the room. Only white men were present at the signing of our nation's foundational documents. This is who our nation's founders believed were equal: white, wealthy men.

In our conversations with the participants of Color School, we pointed out that it's important to get into the head, heart, and lifestyle of Thomas Jefferson to unpack what "all *men* are created equal" meant within his culture and environment. Jefferson's view of *men* was framed in America's aristocratic planter class—white European men like him who were equal in terms of being free, owning property, and having wealth. The Declaration of Independence was a response to the tyrannical rule of King George III and the ongoing war against the British. As our friend, historian Jim Stewart, pointed out on an episode of *Radio in Black and White*, the conversation just before the Revolutionary War was about taxes and the monarchy, not about faith and equality. Our nation's founders wanted to be free of unfair financial burden—"taxation without representation"—and were not eager to secure true freedom for all the people in the colonies. They didn't believe that all the people in the colonies deserved equality or freedom.

As Frederick Douglass asked in a speech in July 1852, "Are the great principles of political freedom and of natural justice, embodied in that Declaration of Independence, extended to us?"[13] The answer to Douglass's question was no, not at all. A few years later in 1857, Roger B. Taney, chief justice of the Supreme Court, writing in the *Dred Scott* decision, said that black people "had no rights which the white man was bound to respect."[14] These are not the words of those living in a society in which equality among races and ethnicities is considered normal.

For much of our nation's history, because of intentional legislation and tacit social systems, it has been impossible for many people of color to achieve basic rights and opportunities. Here, the myth of meritocracy is exposed. If we are white in America, we are taught that with hard work and good ideas, timing, and luck, anyone can bootstrap their way up in a "land of opportunity." But as people in communities of color have often said, "Some boots don't have straps."

When we continue to claim that people get what they work for, and deny that privilege and supremacy are real, we ignore and deny racial disparities that stare back at us across the color line.

- African Americans have a poverty rate of 27.4 percent and Latino Americans a poverty rate of 26.6 percent, compared to a poverty rate of 9.9 percent among European Americans.[15]

- The unemployment rate among African Americans (7.5 percent) is nearly double that of European Americans (3.8 percent).[16]

- Whites continue to dominate America's top jobs, holding 83 percent of all management-level positions, and continue to receive 20 percent higher pay at the same educational levels as their black counterparts.[17]

It can be tempting to read statistics like these and slide into arguments about how "those people" just don't work hard enough or are lazy or like to live off welfare. But these arguments are racist at the core. These statistics reflect the white supremacist nature of our employment structures.

The kind of racism that continues to disadvantage people of color in judicial and job processes "has horrific implications for the political aspirations of people of color," says Bryan Stevenson, executive director of the Equal Justice Initiative and author of *Just Mercy*.[18] It leaves communities traumatized, underserved, and oppressed.

Additionally, census data show that black and brown people are the last hired and first fired and that consistent differences exist in the presence of disease, health outcomes, quality of healthcare, and access to healthcare services across racial and ethnic lines.[19] Add to these injustices the phenomena of DWB (driving while black), SWB (shopping while black), or, in the tragic case of Trayvon Martin, GHWB (going home while black), and we quickly see that we live in nothing like a meritocracy. We live in a supremacy.

The terrible legacy of Plantation Jesus has instilled in millions of oppressed people across generations the "social and economic inferiority" of blacks and the "cultural racism" of whites, says James Loewen in his book *Lies My Teacher Told Me*.[20] What we have inherited from slavery is a core belief that it is "appropriate, even 'natural,' for whites to be on top, blacks on the bottom." With this idea at our center, says Loewen, it's simple to believe that "Europe's domination of the world came about because Europeans were smarter."[21] When all this racist belief is wrapped in a religious and moral package and presented as part of God's divine plan, the impact is devastating. Here, Plantation Jesus is doing his best work.

BREAKING THROUGH THE FOG OF DENIAL

Nearly two centuries after Jefferson's death, supremacy and privilege continue to have an impact on the lives of people of color. Plantation Jesus continues to live in the patterns of bigotry and prejudice.

This is true even in the churches where we have worked and worshiped. When Scott Hagan was installed as senior pastor of our church in Grand Rapids, many changes in worship style and procedure focused on reaching those different from the prevailing European ethnic groups that had dominated the church for decades. Hagan was deeply invested in breaking down white supremacy and bringing not just more true diversity to the congregation but true equality too. One thing Hagan expressed many times was the need to make connections with someone different from ourselves: "Have someone from church over for dinner who doesn't look like you," he often said.

Since a similar process had brought us together as friends, we thought that many people would respond to this opportunity. We were wrong. "Well, I appreciate what Pastor Scott is trying to do," one well-established congregational leader said, "but I'll be damned if I'll bring a nigger into my house." Sadly, this was far from an isolated incident. In fact, many congregation members left the church because of Pastor Hagan's work in this area.

It's hard to comprehend that this kind of straight-up racism came from a person in church leadership. But in some ways it was even more challenging on a personal level to see this kind of poison from people we thought we knew. Every Monday morning, "scud missile" emails, laced with some of the most foul, racist language imaginable, hit the inbox of the music director at our church. Nothing was ever done about these messages. Many churches have disciplinary procedures in place for counselors, deacons, and elders to handle inappropriate behavior. But apparently, at least at that particular church, racism was not on the list of transgressions. When Pastor Hagan left, we were appalled by the number of people who came back to the church. Under a newly installed leader, those who had expressed such vehement racism returned to the congregation without facing any kind of confrontation about their behavior, which had clearly been outside of God's heart and mind. The church, once again, refused to confront the racism in its midst.

Plantation Jesus reigns in churches all over America both by design and by default. While some Christian leaders in the United States talk in platitudes about being "multiracial, multiethnic, and antiracist," churches remain ten times more segregated than the neighborhoods in which they are located, says sociologist Michael Emerson.[22]

The only way we will ever make change is by deconstructing white supremacy and privilege and breaking through the fog of denial. And to do this work, we must recognize the privilege of white people and the system of white supremacy

that keeps that privilege in place. Until we can see it, we cannot change it.

DISCUSSION QUESTIONS

- What was your reaction when you first heard about white privilege and the ideology of white supremacy?

- What manifestations of white supremacy do you see around you?

- Is it difficult for you to hear the real facts about American history? If so, why?

- How does digging into the facts of American history change your identity as an American? As a follower of Jesus?

6

WHO WE WORSHIP
The Myth of America as a Christian Nation

ONE DAY in the late 1950s in Dearborn, Michigan, history penetrated my (Rick's) ignorance about the way that racism and patriotism intersect. A friend and I were exploring his house, and we discovered a treasure trove of World War II memorabilia his dad had collected as a GI in Germany: helmets, medals, uniforms, and two Nazi swastika armbands. In a moment of twelve-year-old spontaneity and stupidity, we decided to don the helmets and armbands and then walk around our neighborhood like goose-stepping Nazis, laughing the whole time.

We hadn't gotten far when an older gentleman came out of his house and called us over. "Could I talk to you for a moment, boys?" he asked in a thick Polish accent. When we nodded, he said, "Do you know the history behind what you're wearing today?"

Then, in five minutes of powerful, eyewitness storytelling, he told us about the Warsaw ghetto and the Nazi death camps at Auschwitz and Treblinka, where he had lost most of his relatives. We listened silently and with growing horror. The neighbor ended his story gently and firmly: "I thought that if you knew what these symbols meant to *me*, you'd find something else to play with."

We walked back to my friend's house in tears, broken-hearted over his story. This man never once yelled at us; he simply told the truth until we understood our own ignorance and how hurtful our play had been. We had never intended any harm, but we had caused it nonetheless. I never forgot that encounter, nor how important it was for me and my friend to understand the impact of our ignorance.

Our intentions are, after all, not the point. The impact of our actions is what's important. We must always understand the difference between intention and impact. "But I meant well" can never be an excuse for hurtful behavior or words. We must listen, acknowledge the harm, even when it was unintended, and pledge to do better.

In recent years, the Confederate battle flag and Confederate monuments have been the subject of much discussion. Many people, including many Southern Christians, have expressed outrage over the removal of Confederate symbols from government buildings like the State House in South Carolina and a public park in Charlottesville, Virginia. Those who support the flag and these monuments claim "heritage" as the reason for their passionate opposition to their removal. They say that the flag expresses something crucial about what it is to be Southern and that these statues are part of history that should be left standing. They say that people are trying to "rewrite history" or "deny that the Civil War ever happened." They claim that people are just trying to stir up trouble.

And across the country, Confederate flags have been showing up more and more often—flown on homes, held at post-election rallies, waved at schools where students tell their Hispanic classmates to "pack their bags" because they're going home. Many people use the Confederate flag as a way of "claiming a white racial identity" even outside the South, says Grace Elizabeth Hale, professor of American studies and history at the University of Virginia.[1]

But most African Americans view Confederate flags, statues, and other paraphernalia from that era quite differently. Time and again, our brothers and sisters of color have told us that these symbols are painful, that these flags and statues call forth the trauma that they have suffered for generations. For many brothers and sisters of color, these symbols are frightening, making them nervous to be in spaces where these flags and monuments hang and stand. Yet many people, even Christians, still hang these flags and battle for these statues, elevating their own beliefs and desires over the feelings and histories of their sisters and brothers of color. Plantation Jesus is a powerful force.

Thus, claims that these symbols are simply heritage symbols or harmless reminders of a lovely past rely on a level of willful ignorance that is almost as astounding as the claim that Thomas Jefferson never owned slaves. As numerous news stories, TV programs, and blog posts have explained, with a great deal of factual evidence: the Confederate battle flag was only erected at public institutions and claimed as part of Southern identity in the 1940s and 1950s, when it was brought forth as a way of setting the South's feet firmly on the foundation of segregation and Jim Crow laws. Likewise, most Confederate monuments were erected in the South during the early part of the twentieth century, when the propaganda around the "glory" of the Confederacy was inextricably tied to the laws of the Jim Crow South.

That being said, the claims that the Confederate battle flag and statues of Confederate generals represent part of Southern heritage are, in fact and sadly, true. But the idea that this heritage is innocent and positive is wrong and dangerous. The history of this flag and the memorials to the Confederacy—from the Confederate position on slavery to the use of the flag in Jim Crow segregation to the flag's presence alongside Nazi swastikas at rallies for hate groups—is tied inextricably to racism.

So no matter how much people intend these symbols to be about appreciating the best things about the Southern way of life, they represent the worst things in Southern history: slavery, segregation, and ongoing racism against African Americans. They perpetuate the psychological harm done to African Americans since the founding of our nation.

Many Christians who don't fly the Confederate flag still subscribe to the sensibilities which imbue that symbol: a belief that America is a "Christian nation," and that we must return to those golden days of yore in which life was better and more moral. Christians have a special responsibility to speak out against these symbols, since Christianity has so often been used to justify and celebrate racial injustice. In this chapter we consider the way that Plantation Jesus has propped up the myth of America as a Christian nation, and what that means for us as Christians today.

THE VALUES PACKAGE

Plantation Jesus has effectively created the "values package": faith, family, ancestry, and country. All these pieces are touted as elements of being a good American Christian. People who buy Plantation Jesus' values package believe that Christianity is essential to true American identity, place the concept of family above all other relationships, accept their privileges as the consequences of "good living" by their ancestors, and believe wholeheartedly in the innate goodness of all things American. We'll unpack each of these a bit more in this chapter.

The package is deceptively appealing. It is overwhelmingly white, nominally Christian, well marketed, and financially successful. But its messaging is profoundly toxic—an unholy alchemy built on a theocratic foundation whose bedrock is America's slaveholding past. Just as Thomas Jefferson was not, in fact, a Bible-believing Christian, America is not—no matter what the values-package proponents might suggest—a Christian nation.

As I (Skot) observed the 2016 presidential election, I began to have serious questions about the faith community's ability to discern the quality of political leadership. Why had so many "values voters" embraced Donald Trump so enthusiastically? We had no definitive proof that Trump is a Christian, although people like James Dobson seemed eager to claim he is.

Even if he is a Christian, do we need our president to share our faith? Or are we misplacing our faith in the work of a nation instead of the work of God? Theologian Stanley Hauerwas cautions that it may be the latter. "Trump is quite pious, and his religious convictions run dangerously deep," Hauerwas writes. "But his piety is not a reflection of a Christian faith. His piety is formed by his understanding of what makes America a country like no other."[2] In other words, Trump is not a man who is devoted to God; Trump is devoted to America. He practices idolatry, or worship of that which is not God. And yet 81 percent of white evangelicals voted for him.

As Wayne Benson, a gifted pastor and Bible teacher, often says in his sermons, the real test of leadership is contained in a simple question: Who do you submit to? "If the answer is 'I submit to no one,'" he says, "then this is a person who is potentially dangerous and should not be followed." Yet so many Christians latched onto Trump's nationalist rhetoric and celebrated the policies and executive orders that stand in direct contradiction to Scripture. If the American church is more interested in promoting xenophobia and racism in the name of patriotism than it is in uplifting the orphan and the widow in the name of Christ, then we are a church of America, not a church of God.

Let's examine the aspects of the values package that have appealed to American Christians and to which they have subscribed.

FAITH AND FAMILY

When Christians talk about our priorities, we sometimes say something like, "We put our faith and our family first." This phrase sounds good, doesn't it? What could be better than faith and family? But sadly, it reveals a cultural Christianity that gives priority to a set of faith practices and a certain group of people rather than giving that priority to God and the direction God would lead us. Further, these concepts of faith and family are often linked, as if putting the welfare of our family first in all situations—even above what God has asked us to do—is an act of faith. In this belief system, good Christians put their family first. Always.

But when we accept the idea that faith and family are not only linked but in many ways synonymous, we are making a graven image of our families. Jesus said, "Do not think that I have come to bring peace to the earth; I have not come to bring peace, but a sword. For I have come to set a man against his father, and a daughter against her mother, and a daughter-in-law against her mother-in-law; and one's foes will be members of one's own household. Whoever loves father or mother more than me is not worthy of me; and whoever loves son or daughter more than me is not worthy of me" (Matthew 10:34-37).

Worship of the nuclear family is part of the mythology that holds sway over much of the Christian church in America. When it's testimony time, our stories often begin with the inevitable "I was born in a Christian home." That phrase—a "Christian home"—can become a platitude devoid of real meaning. What does it mean to have grown up in a Christian home?

In fact, whenever the word *Christian* is used as an adjective, confusion quickly sets in. What does it mean for music, television, bookstores, radio stations, games, or homes to be "Christian"? This comfortable religious and cultural furniture has nothing *necessarily* to do with a personal relationship with Christ, the thing that really makes a person a Christian. As Billy Graham has said, "A Christian is a person who has a relationship with Jesus Christ."[3]

In other words, objects, art, music, nations, even families: these things cannot, in and of themselves, be "Christian." A Christian is a person who follows Christ. But in America, we have co-opted Christ and tried to make his message part of our culture.

When we hallow the role of the "Christian home" or the "Christian family" within a national identity, we get into dangerous territory. Using *Christian* as a descriptor of anything but people who follow Jesus has allowed the term, and Christ himself, to be appropriated for people's own purposes. In fact, when we appropriate the name of Christ as an adjective, and add to that the practice of racism in the United States, we find that Plantation Jesus has focused the idea of "faith and family" on a particular kind of family: the white family. Plantation Jesus overlooks the systematic destruction of black and Native American families. Plantation Jesus holds up the Norman Rockwell painting of white folks gathered at the Thanksgiving table as the paragon of what people who follow Jesus look like.

When we claim that a core element of American life is the "family" but ignore the fact that many American families were intentionally displaced, divided, and oppressed, we further entrench a lie. Not only do we use Christ to settle ourselves into a comfortable culture that is safe and carefully defined in terms of practices and beliefs. We also use him to circumscribe the "right" way of living our faith as being limited to white people, who have historically been more privileged economically and socially. Thus white families have been able to create and maintain dynamics and structures over generations—structures that have not always been available to people of color.

In a compelling book, *Help Me to Find My People: The African American Search for Family Lost in Slavery*, Heather Andrea Williams digs deeply into the experience of race-based chattel bondage in the United States and its impact on family relationships. While doing research on black newspapers that began to be published after the Civil War, Williams found numerous ads from family members looking for loved ones they had lost. "African Americans described with poignant power the grief they felt losing their parents, children, sisters, brothers, husbands, and wives," Williams writes. "In the midst of these jarring separations there were almost always white people—masters, mistresses, traders, auctioneers, purchasers—participants in the separations and witnesses to the pain."[4]

Take an ad that appeared in the *Colored Tennessean* in 1865. It read:

Information is wanted about my two boys, James and Horace, one of whom was sold in Nashville and the other was sold in Rutherford County. I, myself, was sold in Nashville and sent to Alabama. . . . Any information . . . will be thankfully received.[5]

Or consider the experience of Native American parents whose children were sent away to "Indian schools" that were created for the sole purpose of making Native American children more white. Forcibly taken from their families, Native American children were made to cut their hair short, speak English instead of their native tongues, and practice Christianity instead of their own religions.

Here in the twenty-first century, it's hard for most of us to imagine these experiences of separation and loss, and harder still to think of how normal the practice was considered to be. God-fearing Christians with "family values" enslaved people for centuries; missionaries demanded that Native children be sent away to "become white." Our so-called "Christian" government forcibly sterilized hundreds of Mexican American people in California. As Williams says, "White people were ever present and implicated in the vast majority of decisions to sell people or to move them from one part of the country to the other."[6]

Take the average slave trader during the era of slavery. Traders moved from place to place, knowingly separating black family members from each other—even as they were writing to their own families about their love and longing for reconnection if it be the Lord's will. Their unconscionable acts made it impossible for families in slavery to ever see each other again. Yet at the same time, these traders were expressing their personal faith and family values and apparently found no conflict between their work and their own family life.

These slave systems were so ubiquitous—such a layered part of normal reality—that confrontational questions were virtually nonexistent. Almost no one asked, "Do you see the incredible cruelty embedded in this enterprise of yours? Do you know what you're doing to families who want to be together just like you and your family?" We must ask deeper questions about the ways that families have been torn apart, often in the name of faith.

ANCESTRY

The second element of the values package is ancestry. Here, we revere our ancestors and celebrate their legacy. We assume our familial predecessors are the "good people"—those who were God-fearing, respectable, prosperous, influential, and admirable. Through this system of ancestry, we inherit connections to privilege without knowing its foundations, a process that enables good people to still be involved in "systems that do harm," says filmmaker Katrina Browne.[7]

The full facts about our ancestors are often hidden in a familial history that focuses on the "good days" and "a fairytale world of New England." Browne is a case in point. When she read a booklet written by her grandmother, all her beliefs about her family changed. Her grandmother wrote, "I haven't stomach enough to describe the ensuing slave trade."[8] Through the research spurred by this letter, Browne, a descendant of the DeWolf family, discovered that her ancestors were the most prolific slave traders in American history. Through their business, the DeWolf family bought and sold over ten thousand Africans over three generations. This painful, hard information drastically changed how Browne saw her family history.

But rather than keeping this story hidden—as many people are wont to do because of shame over their family's actions—Browne began a mission to expose the details of her family's trade by retracing, with a small group of relatives, the steps of her ancestors. Their experience, captured in her award-winning documentary, *Traces of the Trade: A Story of the Deep North*, is stunning and disturbing.

In the film, Browne describes in minute detail the sophisticated and well-organized enterprise that was the DeWolf family business. They owned banks that financed slave-trading voyages, insurance companies that indemnified them, sugar plantations that produced raw material, barrel-making shops that built rum and sugar containers, and ship-building companies that constructed slave ships. This entire organization operated out of Bristol, Rhode Island, a small town in a small state. From there, the DeWolfs serviced forty slave markets worldwide.

The "good people" of Bristol hid their connections to the trade by sustaining a fairy-tale narrative of the family's business as shipbuilding, farming, insurance, banking, and barrel making. But, of course, their work was far more heinous.

The deplorable conditions on slave ships reveal the heart of the DeWolf enterprise: men, women, and children were stacked end to end and lived in their own excrement, trapped for months in the most foul-smelling, disease-ridden environments imaginable. Layers of hopelessness traumatized millions who died on the way, and millions more lived in perpetual despair as, once on New World soil, they made their way through a race-based chattel system.

This abominable work is the work of "good people," some our ancestors, who wove this slave system into the economic and sociological fabric of American democracy. The institution of slavery reveals the normalization of criminal behavior during the time. It was an ancestral institution so spectacularly cruel and unconscionably brutal that it threatened our very humanity. Yet, as a society, we want to pretend that the impact of the slave trade is over. We had nothing to do with that practice, we say, and we don't benefit from it today. We want to pretend our ancestors were good people in every way because that's easier—easier than dealing with the truth and the heart reckoning that comes when we see it.

We can no longer hide behind our "good people." While the DeWolfs may have had the largest slave-trading enterprise, they have lots of company. Slavery was a family business sustained by people with normal jobs who witnessed both the horrific and the mundane. It spanned from the presidents in the planter class, who enslaved hundreds of human beings, to Episcopal ministers, who enslaved one or two people, to farmers, who owned just a few acres and a couple of people to work beside them on the land. If we are white, our ancestry is likely not the pristine through line of goodness that we may claim. No one living in America today is not benefiting from the national ancestry of slaveholders, because we all live under a government created by enslavers, in an economy built on the foundation of slave wealth, and in a white supremacist system designed to perpetuate human bondage.

Because of this ancestry, African American people are often also denied their own family stories. This reality calls into question the hallowed status of concepts like a "family legacy" or a "legacy of faith." The work of genealogy for black people is far more complicated and full of silence than it is for most white people. These complications and silences arise, almost entirely, from the practice and systems of slavery that denied people the ability to read and write, forbade legally recognized marriages, permitted the rape of enslaved women, split apart families through the sale of human beings, and left their stories to be found in the records of white people who owned them and governments that didn't consider them citizens. When we elevate ancestry as a way to establish a good and wholesome personal identity, we are denying the wretched history of slaveholding that is present in many of our families. We are also excluding many African Americans from the possibility of claiming a "family legacy" or a "heritage of faith," something many consider so crucial to being a good American Christian.

COUNTRY

To the ideas of faith and family and ancestry we add country, the last element of the values package. Many Christians see America as a Christian nation. Everyone from the pilgrims to Ronald Reagan has called the country a shining "city on a hill," appropriating a phrase Jesus assigned to those who followed him (see Matthew 5:14). Again, we idolize our nation rather than give our true worship to God, and we use the word *Christian* for things instead of people. Plantation Jesus has a strong foothold here.

But even if we were to grant that the word *Christian* can be appropriately used as an adjective, we severely lack proof of this identity in our nation's history. If it were possible to have a Christian nation, the founding documents of such a country would include Christian principles. A truly Christian nation would not initiate the enslavement of African people or the genocide of Native Americans. A Christian nation would value equality for all its citizens in all circumstances. But the founding documents of the United States do not include biblical principles. In the name of Manifest Destiny, our nation enslaved and murdered millions of people of color. We have to practice some pretty serious self-delusion and deception to claim a "heritage" of Christianity in our nation.

In recent history, prominent politicians have defended the Christian bona fides of the founders, claiming, in the words of former presidential candidate Michele Bachmann, that they "worked tirelessly to end slavery in the United States."[9] This kind of narrative is developed as proof that the United States is favored by God because it is a Christian nation. In fact, ten of the first twelve presidents owned slaves while in office. So no evidence exists to support this claim.

Additionally, a clear case for Christian influence on the founding documents is difficult to construct. While the Declaration of Independence mentions God as Creator, the framers meant something completely different from the "Judeo-Christian heritage" often tagged on this document. Deism—which was the faith of many founders, including Washington, Jefferson, Ethan Allen, James Monroe, and James Madison—maintains that reason and observation are enough to prove the existence of God. When deists speak of the creator, they are talking of a god who "set the world in motion," so to speak, but who has removed himself from the daily operations of life on this planet. This god is far from the God we as Christians recognize: the Creator who led the Israelites by pillars of fire and cloud, the Father of Jesus, who came to earth to live among us.

Also, significantly, neither the Bible nor Jesus is mentioned at all in either the Declaration or the Constitution. Yet Plantation Jesus has surrounded the "Christian nation" myth with a false sense of the sacred with respect to the founding documents. A fundamental belief of many Americans, including Christians, is that the Constitution of the United States is sacrosanct, perfect and right in every way. However, the Constitution has been amended twenty-seven times and is a work in progress. This was the intention of the founders when they allowed for amendments to the document. In contrast, *truly* sacred texts like the Bible are complete and can't ever be edited or amended.

In fact, not only are the founding documents not Christian or sacred—many people, including abolitionist William Lloyd Garrison, believed the founding documents were corrupt because of an immoral partnership with slavery. Garrison asserted that "incorporating the slave system into the government"—as the Constitution does in several places—produced "a covenant with death, and an agreement with hell."[10] The founding documents were so far from Christian in their creation and intention as to be sinful in their support of the institution of slavery. The idea that our founding documents are somehow underwritten by God—a cornerstone of the beliefs of many politically conservative Christians—simply has no basis in fact.

LOYALTY TO JESUS

The greatest danger of the values package is the powerful alchemy of assumptions we barely notice: the way we put our faith and our family members above Christ, the way we ignore the historical harms that have been done to people of color because we want to protect our ancestors' image; the way we twist the truth to shape the United States into something that is comfortable for us. Sadly, the values package is the default position for many Americans; it's the factory setting of cultural Christianity. It's what we do and believe when we're not thinking.

Plantation Jesus has crafted a "Christian nation," perhaps, but it's one that is comfortable with slavery and genocide. It's hard to see much at all that's Christlike about that.

Yet we have the opportunity to change our focus from hope in our nation to hope in our God: a God who is always good, always just, always merciful, and always loving. After all, our God is the only true hope for healing, for each of us and for our country.

DISCUSSION QUESTIONS

- How are faith and family often paired together?

- How does the idea that America was or is a Christian nation appeal to you? Concern you?

- What might seem threatening to Christians when the idea of America as a Christian nation is challenged? What comfort do people find in this idea that their country is a Christian one?

- What is a Christian home?

- In what ways do you personally benefit from the legacy of slavery in our nation?

7

WHERE IS THE MONEY?
Plantation Economics Today

I N THE 1990s, one of college basketball's all-star stories was that of "the Fab Five," a group of highly talented, African American, freshman players from the University of Michigan who changed the style, culture, and tone of the game forever. This team and these players were enormously popular, generating revenue for the National Collegiate Athletic Association (NCAA) and the university, which also signed a sponsorship deal with Nike.

Sportswriter Mitch Albom describes walking with Fab Five member Chris Webber on State Street and passing the ultimate University of Michigan athletic merchandiser in Ann Arbor, Michigan. Prominently displayed in the front window was a basketball jersey with Webber's name and number for sale for fifty dollars. Webber has never received—and will never

receive—a single dollar from the use of his name and reputa-
tion. The names and talents of student-athletes generate money
everywhere except in their pockets. Sometimes they have to
borrow money for pizza after working tireless hours, traveling
countless miles, and, sacrificing the quality of education that
the NCAA is so quick to tout as the justification for this system.[1]

Athletics draw billions of dollars in multiple revenue
streams for colleges and universities. But the student-athletes
themselves are legally banned from making any income from
their own labor.

Welcome to plantation athletics, where students generate huge revenues for their employers while not getting paid
themselves. "Slavery is indeed gone," Frederick Douglass said,
"but its shadow still lingers over the country and poisons . . .
the moral atmosphere of all sections of the republic."[2]

The economic reality of slave systems forms the toxic
foundation of America, but this reality is virtually unknown
to the rest of us because we have been taught to believe slavery
ended with the Civil War, the Emancipation Proclamation,
and the Thirteenth Amendment. Plantation Jesus has made
white Americans secure in the myth of a real meritocracy,
where everyone gets what they earn. This belief makes it possible to act as if the repercussions of slavery no longer exist
and perpetuates the lie that slavery is over.

As historian John Henrik Clarke wrote, "It is too often
forgotten that when the Europeans gained enough maritime
skills and gunpowder to conquer most of the world, they not
only colonized the bulk of the world's people but they colonized the interpretation of history itself."[3]

Thus, it is not enough to know history (although many of us don't even know that). We must *dissect* history. We must question the interpretation of history that we have been taught. We must remember that most often, history is told by the victors, and we must acknowledge the fact that in American history, the victors have typically been white men.

Until we recognize that the legacy of slavery lives large not only in our culture but in our very economic system, we cannot begin to heal from its harms. These harms continue in the economic system that is foundational to not only government but also culture in the United States. In this chapter, we'll look at college athletics and mass incarceration as just two examples of the many ways this economic system is perpetuated in our society today.

SLAVES AS COMMODITIES

To understand the present-day reality of economics, economics rooted in the plantation system, we need to start in 1705, more than seventy years before the United States officially existed. In that year the Virginia General Assembly decreed that "all Negro, mulatto and Indian slaves within this dominion . . . shall be held to be real estate." Thus the system of slave labor as fundamental to economics began to be codified, and the institution of slavery continued for another 160 years. From the beginning, the idea of American wealth was tied tightly to the idea of slavery and the ownership of other human beings. Real estate referred not only to land but also to people.

Lest we are tempted to downplay the economic impact that slavery had on our nation, consider this: According to calculations by two economics professors, the wealth in slaves held by slaveholders in 1860 and translated into 2016 dollars is $13 trillion. That's 77 percent of the U.S. gross domestic product (GDP) today: 77 percent![4] Slavery formed the clear majority of economic wealth in the United States on the eve of the Civil War. Southern plantation owners—and the United States in general—had a lot of wealth to lose if slavery were to be abolished.

In 1820, Thomas Jefferson recognized this dilemma. "We have the wolf by the ear," he said. "We can neither hold him, nor safely let him go. Justice is in one scale, and self-preservation in the other."[5] Self-preservation won, and the uniquely American business model based on slave labor continued. As Ron Mason, president of the Southern University System, has said, "The Founding fathers made a *conscious decision* to put justice aside and create a business model that required slavery, a system to control and exploit black labor."[6]

Slavery defined American business practices, quickly created unparalleled wealth, and became the foundation of enterprise in the United States. Within the chattel model, slaveholders developed processes to access and protect their investments, including "new accounting methods that incorporated (human) property depreciation in the bottom line as slaves aged, as well as new actuarial techniques to indemnify slaveholders from loss or damage to the men and women they owned," write historians Sven Beckert and Seth Rockman.[7] In every way, enslaved people were treated as commodities that depreciated with age and use and that needed to be insured against loss or damage. We can conceive of this most readily, perhaps, by recalling that our cars depreciate in value and have to be insured. Human beings treated like vehicles. That's the bottom line.

Some of America's most successful and well-known companies, including Lehman Brothers, Aetna, JP Morgan Chase, New York Life, Norfolk Southern Railroad, USA Today, and Brooks Brothers, have admitted to profits generated from slave trade activity.[8] Considering the direct and indirect involvement of banks, insurance companies, investment firms, communication entities, transportation, and retail stores, a fair question emerges: Who was *not* involved?

THE PEONAGE SYSTEM

Then came the chaotic and vulnerable time just after the Civil War. In 1865, as the war officially ended, the Southern planter class was affected by one of the greatest government land grabs in world history. The Union government divided up millions of acres in the former Confederacy because the landowners had not paid federal taxes during the war. In some cases, these lands were leased to northerners or Army officers, and then formerly enslaved individuals were hired to work the land. The planters may have been able to bear losing their class identity as landed gentry. But when these wealthy men also lost their power to use slave labor and found themselves having to pay people to work for them, the original foundation of the American economic system—the foundation of slave labor—was disrupted.

Indeed, understanding that a vast proportion of America's wealth came from slavery enables us to understand how drastic a shift in practice and policy was required when the realities of emancipation arrived in 1865 at the conclusion of the Civil War. America's new and growing mines and factories needed cheap labor to sustain huge profits, but the owners of these places could not own slaves anymore. Farmers still had vast tracts of land that needed to be tended, and their workforce now had the choice to work elsewhere. A new system had to be found, and local sheriffs stepped into the power vacuum that the planter class had vacated and create a peonage system that replaced slavery as the labor engine: the convict leasing system and sharecropping.

In *Slavery by Another Name: The Re-enslavement of Black Americans from the Civil War to World War II*, Douglas Blackmon describes in stunning, intimate detail how large corporations involved in lumber, coal mining, and steel production established an arrangement with counties that always had the ability to supply cheap labor literally on demand. As companies like U.S. Steel let officials know how much labor they needed, local sheriffs began to arrest black men on charges like vagrancy, wearing the wrong kind of clothes, or saying the wrong thing to a white person. Fines and fees accrued as these capricious, arbitrary charges worked their way through court systems, and when the accused were unable to pay, they were ultimately charged with a period of hard labor. Firms then paid these fines to the county, which in turn left the accused in corporate hands, for whom they worked to pay off their debts.

What evolved was a peonage system that bound a debtor (the "peon") to a creditor until his or her debts were paid. What made this system "slavery by another name" was the

nefarious, race-based, supply-and-demand arrangement between companies and county governments. If you were black
and poor and lived in the southern United States anytime between the end of the Civil War and World War II, you were
caught in hard-labor purgatory. Even if you worked off your
debt and the company set you free, as a former prisoner with
few rights or opportunities, you could—and likely would—
be caught up in the process again. You would be charged with
vagrancy or improper clothing, and at the whim of law en-
forcement and the needs of mining and manufacturing, the
pattern would continue.

It is hard to imagine how horrific the conditions were
in these facilities. The housing was disease-ridden, and the
overseers were consistently cruel and practiced unusual
punishment. Men were often literally worked to death. The
peonage system is one baleful legacy of slavery's business
model of powering American profits by exploiting and con-
trolling black labor in the heart of the Bible Belt. This peonage era in the long history of racism, and the economic
oppression that was often its result, continued well into the
twentieth century.

PLANTATION ECONOMICS TODAY

We hold a lot of misconceptions about the relevance of history. The cliché we hear most often is a statement that becomes
what we have labeled a conversation stopper, a statement
rooted in ignorance and insensitivity. "Well, that slavery and
Jim Crow stuff was a long time ago," white folks often say. Or,
"That was then and this is now." Or, "We just need to get past

all this and move on." These are other versions of the "Get over it" phrase that we unpacked in chapter 1.

Plantation Jesus loves this kind of dismissive dialogue, because the conversation is over before it even begins. If something happened "a long time ago," then surely it can have no relevance or impact today. Why even bother discussing it? Ironically, this dismissal of history is often articulated by the same people who proclaim that their ancestors were heroes for fighting in long-ago wars and who still stake a great deal of pride on their family's legacy in a certain place. It appears, then, that "moving on" is only necessary if the history in question does not reflect particularly well on you or your people.

Some people want to act as if slavery is "long dead." Yet slavery's shadow remains, especially in the realm of economics. Historians have taught us to see history as a series of patterns that continue to repeat themselves over epochs of time. Thus, what happened in 1776 is very relevant to the twenty-first century—not in the vague, romantic mythology of "founding principles" but in the stone-cold reality of an American business model that is still dependent on slave labor, performed by people of color who must be controlled so that they can be exploited. Even in the twenty-first century, we still find enormous profits being generated for wealthy "plantation owners" by more subtle but no less evil and insidious forms of slave labor. Let's consider some examples.

COLLEGE ATHLETICS

For one of many examples, look no further than the NCAA. Every year the NCAA designs and organizes what is arguably one of the greatest sports spectacles on television: a basket-ball tournament involving sixty-eight teams that draws more than 140 million viewers. March Madness is second in rat-ings only to the Super Bowl, and the revenues are stagger-ing. The current fourteen-year NCAA contract with CBS and Turner Broadcasting is worth $10.8 billion.[9] This does not include ticket sales to tournament games, sales of sports gear, revenue from the sale of recordings of past games to other sports networks, video games that commonly use the images of former players, and endorsement deals from companies like Nike and Adidas. The coaches, administrators, network executives, video game producers, and the NCAA itself are also doing very well with compensation packages, which are at well more than $2–$3 million at the executive level.

However, the students—the athletes whose labor is earn-ing these spectacular figures—are not compensated at all. NCAA regulations ban athletes from receiving any sort of payment, in cash or goods, for their labor. If they are found to have accepted payment—even small payments for things like promising to remain with a particular agent when they go professional—they lose their NCAA eligibility. This means they lose their place on the team and thus, quite often, the ath-letic scholarship that allowed them to attend that university.

"You've got a labor force that is essentially indentured servants. It's pretty convenient if you don't have to pay the players," says Michael Lewis, author of *The Blind Side*.[10] No athletic competition is possible in any school supervised by the NCAA without the student signing a form that prohib-its any manner of compensation for playing. This form also gives the governing body rights to the player's image, name, and past game footage.

The NCAA system exploits all student-athletes, but when you consider that almost 25 percent of all male student-athletes and 16 percent of all female student-athletes are black, as compared to the general population in which 12.6 percent of Americans are black, larger questions emerge.[11] The system takes advantage of already underprivileged African American people in our country by offering scholarships for athletics, taking advantage of that person's athletic ability for another's gain, and then failing to deliver on even the flimsy promise of education offered through scholarship. In the 2016-2017 academic year, 44.5 percent of male college basketball players and 31.5 percent of female basketball players were black. During that same period, 38.7 percent of college football players were black.[12] Two of the most popular revenue-generating sports in the United States were played by teams where over a third of the players were black people: black people who were not paid for their labor.

The NCAA counters the argument that the athletes are working in a new form of slave labor by pointing to athletic scholarships and claiming that these scholarships allow students a chance to get an education. Yet, to use college football as an example, only 50 percent of black student football players graduate in six years. So much for the effectiveness of those scholarships in getting students a good education. Additionally, most scholarships are awarded on a one-year basis; if players are no longer valuable to a team, they are cut. Gone and forgotten.

Consider, too, the vast inequality between student scholarships and institutional earnings. Male Division I athletes were awarded an average of $14,270 in scholarships during 2015; female Division I athletes received an average of $15,162. The total value of those scholarships was $2.2 billion.[13] But in the same year, NCAA Division I schools earned $9.15 billion from athletics.[14]

Take Texas A&M University, the school with the highest revenues from student-athletes' labor. The school athletics programs brought in $192.6 million in revenue in 2016, and on average, their male athletes collected $13,557 and their female athletes $12,856 in scholarships.[15] That means that, on average, each of their student-athletes earned 0.00686 percent of the total revenue in scholarships. The NCAA schools are exploiting their student-athletes and using their labor to fund the university's lifestyle. This is plantation economics, pure and simple.

In an America that ostensibly values equality and fairness, someone should begin to ask questions about this collegiate brand of plantation economics. Why can't these universities at least provide high-risk health insurance more suitable to the needs of student-athletes? The echoes of the plantation are disturbing.

Within the historical pattern that Plantation Jesus put in place when our country was founded and that continues to be perpetuated through people who are not willing to see the truth, it's just too easy to oppress and exploit the dreams of a free labor force who believes that one day they can play in the NFL or the NBA. The cold reality is that less than 1 percent of student-athletes will ever sign a professional contract. Still, the NCAA continues to exploit students who may have few other options to enter college by promising them a scholarship and education that could lead to "big things." The NCAA and college athletics remain big business, relying on free labor from poor kids of color whose "hope is eternal, and their ignorance exploitable."[16]

ESPN basketball analyst Jay Bilas calls the current NCAA system "profoundly immoral." In an interview with the *Wall Street Journal*, Bilas said, "What's really happening is the schools are selling the athletes . . . and they're keeping all the money." The students are told, "You're an amateur, this is what college sports is all about." But, says Bilas, that's not what it's about for coaches, administrators, and presidents. The operating principle is "I benefit, you get nothing, and if you violate our rules . . . we'll make you look like a criminal."[17] Recently, Chris Webber of the Fab Five said, "I definitely think student-athletes have the right to make sure they can take care of each other. You know, Bill Russell told me any system that gets free labor is slavery."[18]

Plantation Jesus is content to leave slave systems in place and keep most Americans in ignorance. The auction blocks have been replaced by basketball courts, football fields, and baseball diamonds. A disproportionately black and brown labor force continues to participate in well-worn economic patterns of exploitation.

MASS INCARCERATION AND PRIVATE PRISONS

Not only does plantation economics show up in college athletics—it also functions in America's prison-industrial complex. In the United States today, 60 percent of the people in prisons are people of color, and 75 percent of all people in state prisons for drug conviction are people of color—despite the fact that rates of drug use are the same across the racial spectrum.[19]

But it's not just the racist nature of incarceration that's at play here: prisons are big moneymakers. Nearly $80 billion is spent on prisons each year.[20] Additionally, according to the U.S. Department of Education, "from 1989–90 to 2012–13, state and local spending on corrections rose by 89 percent while state and local appropriations for higher education remained flat."[21] We clearly are more interested, as a nation, in imprisoning people, particularly people of color, than we are in providing education and training that could improve lives.

As Michelle Alexander argues in her book *The New Jim Crow: Mass Incarceration in the Age of Colorblindness*, "Mass incarceration in the United States . . . emerged as a stunningly comprehensive and well-disguised system of racialized social control that functions in a manner strikingly similar to Jim Crow."[22] Even as the work of the civil rights movement was beginning to break down the overt legal systems that oppressed people of color in the United States, Alexander argues, others were working to put in place a "law and order" system that could covertly re-create a system of racial castes using the criminal justice system. This belief in the need for "law and order," along with the presidential war on drugs that began in the 1980s, has led to a new racist system that operates quietly. Without direct reference to race, it continues to subjugate people of color, particularly black and brown men.

Couple this quiet racism with the vast amount of profit that the prison industry earns each year, and we begin to understand why people are so invested in imprisoning people, particularly people of color who have less political and social power because of our long history of systemic racism. Prison is big business for the private prisons that continually lobby federal and state governments for lengthier sentences for crimes, because those longer sentences mean that the government pays them more. It is big business for the various industries that make money from the prison system: prison phone companies, prison healthcare providers, commissaries that provide food for prisoners, for-profit bail bond companies, and on and on. According to journalist Eric Markowitz, these private industries that work within prisons bring in well over $5.5 billion a year—and that's just from the industries whose figures Markowitz was able to approximate. It's no wonder so many people have a vested interest in keeping as many people as possible in prison as long as possible. There's a lot of money to be made—and lost.

It was exactly this loss of wealth that kept so many Southern plantation owners committed to the cause of slavery, even when they had moral objections. Take, for example, James Madison, framer of the U.S. Constitution and our fourth president. Madison wrote publicly and frequently about how much he detested the practice of slavery. Yet he never freed any of the at least 119 people he enslaved at his Virginia plantation. It was too great a risk to his wealth. This was the case with almost every slaveholder in the United States.

Today, in the exact landscapes of enslavement—many prisons are built on former plantations—prisons re-create slave systems in many ways. They deny individuals freedom of movement and choice, they disenfranchise people who are caught up in the system, they target people of color, they break apart families, and they stigmatize people who have been part of that system, all codified in language of "law and order" that acts as a mask for racism and profit.

These patterns of plantation economics are visible in many spheres, including the uproar around NFL player Colin Kaepernick and his peaceful protest during the national anthem, beginning in 2016. As a result of his actions, no team would sign him in the 2017 season—but white athletes who are found guilty of spousal abuse have no trouble being picked up for a new season.

As long as Plantation Jesus continues to blind our eyes and blunt our empathy, nothing will change and the patterns will continue. These things are not history from "way back when," stories from a bygone era that holds only nostalgia and no power. These are realities of today, realities that we very literally buy into with our dollars. These are realities that we must first see and then change.

Discussion questions

- Where do you see plantation economic systems at work?
- In what ways might you unknowingly support the

exploitation of people of color through athletics or the
system of mass incarceration?

- How do you recognize exploitation? How can you stop it?
- Discuss who is hurt by plantation economics.

8

WHERE DO WE GO FROM HERE?
Following the Real Jesus

I N AUGUST 1967, just a few months before he was
assassinated, Martin Luther King Jr. delivered his speech
"Where Do We Go from Here?" at the eleventh annual convention of the Southern Christian Leadership Conference. In
that speech, he said,

> And so we still have a long, long way to go before we reach
> the promised land of freedom. Yes, we have left the dusty soils
> of Egypt, and we have crossed a Red Sea that had for years been
> hardened by a long and piercing winter of massive resistance,
> but before we reach the majestic shores of the promised land,
> there will still be gigantic mountains of opposition ahead and
> prodigious hilltops of injustice. We still need some Paul Reveres

138 / PLANTATION JESUS

of conscience to alert every hamlet and every village of America that revolution is still at hand. Yes, we need a chart; we need a compass; indeed, we need some North Star to guide us into a future shrouded with impenetrable uncertainties.[1]

King's call echoes through the years to the churches of the United States, a country that is still so racially divided and is still living out the legacy of slavery in manifold ways. Churches can be incubators of justice, carriers of compassion, and communities of resistance. We can be the Paul Reveres of conscience. We can follow our North Star, our compass: the real Jesus. Jesus Christ, who walked this earth in human form, who knew our struggles and our brokenness as our brother and our friend. Plantation Jesus is the false construct, the god who is comfortable with oppression and injustice. Jesus of Nazareth is the real Jesus—the Jesus we must follow and worship and the Jesus who helps us identify the false gods our nation offers to us.

WHO IS THE REAL JESUS?

The real Jesus did not participate in systems of oppression; he stood in direct opposition to them, even when it cost him his life. The real Jesus did not kowtow to systems that said some people were more valuable than others; he invited everyone to his table. The real Jesus did not tell people to get over their pain; he sat with them in it and healed them of it. The real Jesus held everyone equal, everyone valuable, everyone worth loving.

The real Jesus knew what it was to be in a position of power over others—supreme, sovereign power, in fact—and yet he never took advantage of that power. Philippians says that as Jesus emptied himself of power, "he humbled himself and became obedient to the point of death—even death on a cross" (Philippians 2:8). He came down from heaven and got into the dirt of life with us, placing his fingers in it to heal, to forgive, to love.

In the gospel of John, we read the story of Jesus and the Samaritan woman at the well. Jesus, as a Jew, was expected to not have any social contact with Samaritans, a group of people with whom the Jews had been at odds—despite their common ancestry—for centuries. But Jesus did not hold with those systemic practices of separation and oppression. Instead, he called the Samaritan woman closer and asked her to share with him. Then, in a way only the Son of God could—a way that was without shame—he called her to belief in healing, the healing only he could offer, by telling her of himself, the Living Water. He paid no mind to what society said about his ethnic supremacy. Instead, he saw her fully as who she was in every way and gave her healing hope, because he knew he was the only one who could.

Jesus also knew what it was to be oppressed. As the Son of God, he became a prisoner, a victim. He could have easily avoided that experience, but he knew his life would serve a purpose beyond simply power, or at least power as we understand it.

As he stood before Pilate, he answered only one question: "Are you the king of the Jews?" Jesus simply replied, "You say so" (Luke 23:3). He owned his ethnicity—he didn't try to pretend he was not a Jew—and did not cower in the face of

Roman power. Nor did he flinch when his own people, the Jewish leadership, refused to save him when Pilate offered up Barabbas. Instead, he submitted to arrest, torture, and ultimately death, but not simply for the sake of submission. Nothing about being a part of God's kingdom work calls for the willful submission to any authority but God. Rather, Jesus submitted so that he might subvert the systems of life and death, and thus overcome death for us all. He took the power of the oppressor and turned it on its head.

The real Jesus comes down from his high place. The real Jesus gets close to people. He pulls children onto his knee and kneels in the dirt with a woman about to be stoned. He mixes his saliva with earth to heal the eyes of the blind and invites everyone through the same door to dine with him. He joyfully accepts the gift of expensive perfume poured out on his feet and takes the hand of a man slipping below the waves. He washes the feet of the people he loves and sits at the table to eat with them. He stands among his workers, bending his back to the work with them, and proclaims himself one of them even as he is also their hope for a way out.

Following the real Jesus into the work of racial and ethnic reconciliation is a challenge. It requires risk and change and the willingness to let go of some of our comforts and privileges, even on Sunday morning. As God's church, we are not always good at risk and change; we are not always good at discomfort. But we can be. We can do the hard work of change and inclusion if we choose to do it deliberately and with a clear focus on God's leading.

CHURCHES FINDING A NEW WAY FORWARD

So how can the American church loosen its allegiance to Plantation Jesus and remember its true identity in Christ? Many congregations are modeling the way for us.

Consider the work of Stones Church in Grand Rapids, Michigan, my (Skot's) home church family. We have taken on this mission:

> We believe that it is your personal relationship with God that positions you for the maximum life possible. We also exist to break down barriers that have been built between people; racial, gender, denominational, class, cultural, etc. We believe that God has given us the authority, access, and commission to establish heaven's values on earth.
>
> We as a congregation are pressing toward looking more like the kingdom of God by seeking God and the full life of God's kingdom. We don't necessarily focus on diversifying the ethnic and racial makeup of our congregation; the commonality in membership is simply people who are hungry for God's presence. Period. We focus on God's leading, on presence over programs, and on encouraging people to represent God's kingdom, whoever and wherever they are.[2]

In the rich cultural waters of San Francisco, St. John's Presbyterian Church is seeking to represent God's kingdom as it is represented in their community. While they have done some of the most common—and, Pastor Theresa Cho would argue, less effective—tactics like hiring a minister of color (Cho was that minister), she says,

What I find to be more effective is to address the emotions, concepts, and characteristics of the congregation that are prohibitive for a diverse community to thrive. For St. John's, this began with welcoming children in worship. Having children in worship addressed the same discomfort and emotions that any diversity would bring. Kids worship differently. They see God differently. Their presence demands worship to change in the way God's word is revealed via music, preaching, and rituals. The presence of kids can pull on how adults believe worship should be: quiet, proper, still, organized, well-executed. Kids are messy, loud, unpredictable, and forthcoming. Therefore, having kids in worship is just as important for the adults as it is for the kids. Kids in worship teach us and allow us to practice patience, grace, forgiveness, unconditional love, nurture.

As we practiced these God-given actions with the kids, we found ourselves changing—our capacity to be flexible and let go increasing. This overflowed to other people. Slowly, over time, not only children felt welcomed, but people of other racial ethnic diversity as well.

Starting with something small, like inviting children into worship, allows people to shift toward bigger, harder changes.[3]

First Baptist Church Ashland in Virginia has taken a similar tack to St. John's by "starting small," as Pastor Sean Hamon says. "That perfect opportunity [to start small] was present in our church community already—our worship service." The congregation combined two services, neither of which was well-attended or vibrant, into one service. "This may seem trivial," Hamon says, "but during our process we realized that everyone has to give up some degree of their preferences in order to allow others to have some of their preferences met. We worked on a 75 percent rule. If you are 'happy' more than

75 percent of the time, there is probably something wrong. Not to say that we want unhappy people, but at least 25 percent of the time we should be able to lay aside our own ways to allow others to have their way. This is the model of Christ."[4]

First Baptist Ashland is largely "white, affluent, and conservative," says Hamon. "[Congregants] have become entrenched in these values without even realizing it. There was not room at the table for anyone who wasn't like them. But by raising their awareness of some of these behaviors with a simpler, more palatable experience (worship service preferences), we were able to dive into the deeper waters of race." The church community has begun to see people go out of their way to welcome people who are not like them. They are starting to attend to the things God cares deeply about.[5]

At All Souls Unitarian Church in Tulsa, Oklahoma, the congregation has been at this work for over fifty years. When the Selma to Montgomery March was happening, All Souls held a citywide service in support of the march, and in that experience, their mission for racial justice and reconciliation was born. Since then, they have become one of the most ethnically and racially diverse congregations in Tulsa. In a personal email, member Brian Cordova says that by being a part of this church, "I have learned that God's love is equal for all."[6]

For the members at Harrisburg Brethren in Christ Church in Pennsylvania, the process began many years ago when the church committed to staying in their city neighborhood even as they outgrew their building. During that time, they made a renewed commitment to the ethnically and racially diverse

community in which they were located. Member Peggy
Mumper describes their process this way:

A. Prayed.

B. Sought a vision for our congregation. "Our vision is to be
a thriving, diverse, urban church sharing Christ's love and serv-
ing the needs of our local and global communities."

C. Talked about it from the pulpit. The pastor taught on
the scriptural basis for the church to seek reconciliation and
integration.

D. Lost some people who didn't see why it was a big deal.
Gained people who were excited by it.

E. Hired staff to reflect diversity. Brought more diversity to
the pulpit. Gained understanding of the importance of hierarchy of leadership in various cultures. Screwed things up, apolo-
gized, moved forward again.

F. Grew worship teams to be more diverse and to embrace
a broader spectrum of music. Lost people who didn't like this;
gained others who did.

G. Offered classes on racial reconciliation (a 101-level course
based on the book *More Than Equals*; a 201-level course based on
the book *The Color of Wealth*). Classes were co-taught by a white
person and an African American person. Classes were composed
of whites and blacks. Wore out the small population of black people by asking them to attend these classes, be on worship teams,
and serve on boards and committees.

H. Paid more attention (e.g., celebrated African American
history month, invited more black leaders to preach and teach,
and made congregants aware of opportunities to learn). Had a
jazz/gospel worship service on a Sunday morning.

I. Struggled, struggled, struggled to make our worship music
diverse and good. Still struggling.[7]

Harrisburg Brethren in Christ made a commitment years ago, and they are following through on it, mistakes and all. And it's working. The church was once an almost all-white congregation. Today their membership is much more reflective not only of the community of which they are a part but of God's kingdom in general.

This work of racial justice, as we have said, is hard, and not all churches are successful. Lia Scholl of Wake Forest Baptist Church in Winston-Salem, North Carolina, pastors an almost all-white, liberal congregation. She notes, "In the liberal church, we don't believe we're racist." Scholl had a white parishioner tell her that church was the only place that she didn't have to "put on a mask," a sentiment that reveals just how much privilege some of us well-intentioned Christians carry around. But as Scholl says of white people, "We can't own our culture as long as we are the oppressor." She is committed to this work, but it's a challenge. A deep challenge.[8]

In addition to congregations, some denominations are accepting the challenge. The African Methodist Episcopal Church, for example, made a statement in the wake of the white supremacist rally in Charlottesville in August 2017 to reaffirm their church's "opposition to hate crimes, racism and anti-Semitism, and call[ed] upon the nation, particularly our national leadership, to condemn racism and hatred."[9] The Progressive National Baptist Convention continues the legacy of Martin Luther King Jr. by their continued work for "full voter registration, education and participation in society, economic empowerment and development, and the realization of universal human rights and total human liberation for all people."[10] And the Evangelical Covenant Church has a Racial Righteousness initiative, as well as an Intercultural Development ministry, as part of their larger Love Mercy Do Justice ministry. The Racial Righteousness initiative develops tools and experiences to answer the question, "Is the church effectively reflecting the vision of the kingdom of God in accordance with Revelation 7:9?" The Sankofa Journey, an "interactive experience [that] explores historic sites of importance in the Civil Rights movement and sites of oppression and inequality for people of color, while seeking to move participants toward healing the wounds and racial divide caused by hundreds of years of racial injustice in the United States," is one aspect of this work.[11] The Intercultural Development work of the Covenant denomination equips congregations to "embrace the mosaic of God's kingdom, learning how to engage in mutual exchange and share life with people across ethnicity and culture."[12]

Many organizations also exist to help churches as we find our way forward in this work. Coming to the Table (CTTT) is a national organization dedicated to healing the wounds left by slavery. Through local groups, a biannual national gathering, and print and online resources, CTTT helps churches and individual Christians come to see the truth of how racism operates in our society and invites us all to connect to one another in a mutual journey of racial healing.

The Table Setters is a faith-based nonprofit that hosts events which nurture long-term diverse relationships in churches, schools, and civic institutions. Congregations might also reach out to Arrabon, a Virginia-based ministry that believes "the Church should be a foretaste of a reconciled heaven to our divided world." Arrabon "equip[s] Christian leaders and their communities with the resources to increase their cultural intelligence to effectively participate in reconciliation."[13] By providing organizations with speakers and training, including an eighteen-month-long program, Arrabon walks with groups that want to begin the important work of healing across racial lines.

ACCEPTING THE CHALLENGE

Sisters and brothers, we as churches have to accept the challenge of confronting and overturning racial injustice. We all have to put aside some of our comfort, some of our preferences— be they for a certain order of worship, certain styles of music, certain translations of Scripture, or simply the desire to be among people who don't challenge us personally. We need to challenge our own opinions about individuals that come from our own stereotyped thinking about a racial, ethnic, or social group, and we need to do the work of justice that begins to break down systems of oppression, be they through our entertainment or our politics. That is the work of God in the church: to step beyond our own ease into the experiences of other people and to see God in those faces.

God calls us to this hard work—this work in the fields as God's laborers. In Matthew 9:37-38, Jesus says, "The harvest is plentiful, but the laborers are few; therefore ask the Lord of the harvest to send out laborers into his harvest." We often read this verse to be about evangelism only. But our job isn't only to win souls: it's to be a part of God's work to bind up wounds and mend souls, to repair broken relationships and soothe hearts. We need more workers . . . and we are called to be those workers. As Pastor Sean Hamon says, "There has to be more to being a believer than just following a set of rules and regulations. There has to be a deeper love of what Jesus loves."[14] And Jesus loves all of us, no matter what demographic label we might place on ourselves or others.

When we do this work of healing and mending and loving, we not only step fully into the work that God is doing to bring about God's kingdom; we also harvest the good things of God's way in our lives. Pastor Theresa Cho says that in this work we gain a wider view of God's kingdom, as well as a fresh look at God's Word when we begin to understand it through others' experiences. As Hamon says, "Diversity has shown us the value of all people," which of course is the way God sees us all.[15] Peggy Mumper says of their work at Harrisburg Brethren in Christ, "I and so many other white people have had our eyes opened to some of the struggles facing our brothers and sisters of color and, therefore, us." She also says, "We more closely resemble heaven."[16] As followers of Christ, we always need to do God's will, even if we don't know exactly how to do it. But we can also trust that God has God's good reasons for this work, reasons that work for our good.

We can trust in and learn to follow the real Jesus: the man who walked among us, who knelt in the dirt to write words at our feet. The man who climbed the mountain to pray alone. The man who took a nap in the back of a boat in a stormy sea. The man who was betrayed by his friends who could not stay awake on the last night of his freedom. The man who submitted to far more than just discomfort over music he didn't like or a style of preaching that didn't suit his preferences. The man who submitted to authorities who really had no authority over him, who handed over his life to show us that life and death are in his control, the man who took to a cross to show us what it is to love everyone—every single one of us. That man knows we are all made stronger, richer, wiser, more compassionate, and more loving when we know—as friends, neighbors, brothers, and sisters—the people who look, worship, pray, and sing differently than we do.

At the funeral for Rev. Clementa Pinckney, who was killed by self-avowed white supremacist Dylann Roof while at a prayer meeting at Pinckney's church, Mother Emanuel African Methodist Episcopal Church in Charleston, South Carolina, then-president Barack Obama said,

> Over the course of centuries, black churches served as hush harbors, where slaves could worship in safety, praise houses, where their free descendants could gather and shout "Hallelujah," rest stops for the weary along the Underground Railroad, bunkers for the foot soldiers of the civil rights movement.
>
> They have been and continue to be community centers where we organize for jobs and justice, places of scholarship and network, places where children are loved and fed and kept out of harm's way and told that they are beautiful and smart and taught that they matter.
>
> That's what happens in church. That's what the black church means—our beating heart, the place where our dignity as a people is inviolate.
>
> There's no better example of this tradition than Mother Emanuel, a church built by blacks seeking liberty, burned to the

ground because its founders sought to end slavery, only to rise up again, a phoenix from these ashes.

When there were laws banning all-black church gatherings, services happened here anyway, in defiance of unjust laws. When there was a righteous movement to dismantle Jim Crow, Dr. Martin Luther King Jr. preached from its pulpit, and marches began from its steps.

A sacred place, this church, not just for blacks, not just for Christians, but for every American who cares about the steady expansion of human rights and human dignity in this country; a foundation stone for liberty and justice for all.

That's what the church meant.[17]

That's what we are supposed to be: a sacred place that cares about the humanity and the dignity of everyone around us. May we follow the example of Mother Emanuel and the other congregations that do the good work of justice and the gracious work of mercy.

To be in real relationships across ethnic and racial lines; to stand in solidarity with our brothers and sisters of color when they suffer under white supremacy and fall victim to its deception and insidious nature; to hold grace and forgiveness for our white brothers and sisters when they slip into their own invisible velvet noose that masquerades as privilege—a snare they try to protect; to find ways to forgive each other; to look on one another with love even when we wound each other and know we will inflict those wounds again: that is the work of God. That is holy work. That is the work of the real Jesus, the Jesus who is, even now, overturning the power of Plantation Jesus, every day in every place.

The real Jesus abides with the suffering of his people but will not suffer the existence of systems that perpetuate it. He is the healer, the hope, the one who turns over the tables of oppression. He provides no justification for injustice, only the way out from it. The real Jesus sees the pain of our past, honors it, and travels with us as we heal from it. He does not believe in national or political boundaries; he believes only in the faithful allegiance of his people to himself. He loves the troublemakers and the silent ones. The antifascists and the Nazis. The people who know Black Lives Matter, and those who say that All Lives Matter. The people who want their service to stay three hymns and a sermon until he returns, and those who think worship only happens with a drum set and a bass guitar. The people who hold tightly to the King James translation, and those for whom *The Message* speaks truth most clearly. The people who think church should happen in small groups in tiny buildings, and those who gather in auditoriums that seat thousands. The people who are committed to social justice, and those who don't even know what that phrase means. Jesus loves those of us who wish we could just "get over it," and those who think they never will.

But Jesus will not hold with systems that oppress any of the people he loves. Not ever. The real Jesus is the God of equity and equality, the God of justice and mercy, the God of hope and healing. He is the only God who reigns, and his kingdom will come.

Our choice, then, is this: Who will we follow? Plantation Jesus or the real Jesus? A cruel master who subjugates us all by subjugating a few, or the true Lord who lifts us all up and loves us even in our broken, wounded selves? Will we be a part of the work of God's kingdom? Or will we set our comfort, our shame, our conceptions of our nation, and our political allegiances ahead of God's work?

Our prayer is that we will all choose the healer of hearts and the smasher of systems. Every day. For all our lives long.

RESOURCES AND EXERCISES

IN THESE PAGES, we've explored a lot of what is broken in our understanding of God's kingdom as it relates to race and ethnicity because we believe that it is necessary to acknowledge and see the wounds in order to begin to heal them.

But now that we've brought the light to our injuries, we'd like to offer some ways forward—practical steps that you can take on your own, with your friends or family, or in your church. We pray that through these practical ideas, you can begin to discover your own wounds and the ways you may be wounding others, and thus begin to heal. Sometimes, it can feel overwhelming to recognize injustice and inequity. What can one person do to respond to decades of historical harm? Our hope is that this section will answer that question.

While the first steps to healing are learning, seeing, and understanding, we also know that if we don't take what we've learned, seen, and understood to then seek after change, we are but resounding gongs and clanging cymbals. If we see but do not seek change, then we talk the talk but don't walk the walk of love.

In each section below, we provide an exercise or two that you can undertake on your own or with a group to help you explore the topics of each of the chapters in this book. Our prayer is that you may begin to see how Plantation Jesus has been given space in our Christian community's life and that you may begin to explore ways to shut him out and make more room for the true Jesus.

One more note about these exercises: they can be challenging, and they are bound to bring up some painful, hard things about ourselves and the people we love. It is also very likely that we will make mistakes and say some hurtful things in the process of coming to awareness about our own struggles with racism and prejudice. But that's not a reason to refrain from moving forward in God's good work to further God's kingdom.

We have found the following practices, set out by an organization called Coming to the Table, to be helpful in discussions of this nature.

- Recognize that these conversations are difficult but that everyone comes with the best intentions for the work.
- Acknowledge when we have been hurt by something said by saying a simple "Ouch."

- When someone expresses hurt, the conversation pauses to let the person who was hurt explain and the person who has caused the harm to hear and respond.

- Give grace to everyone involved, including ourselves, without allowing space for racism and prejudice in the conversation.[1]

LEARNING TO RECOGNIZE WHAT WE WERE TAUGHT ABOUT RACE AND ETHNICITY

Circle Up

In this exercise, you will explore the influences that people, places, and events have had on your life and look at them critically with an eye to see what they taught you that was positive and what wasn't so ideal.

1. Put your name in the middle of a sheet of paper.

2. Draw eight circles around your name.

3. In each of those eight circles, write one word that describes a person, place, or event that has had profound impact on your life.

4. Now draw another group of eight circles around each of those first eight and write one word in each of the new circles to describe one thing that this person, place, or event taught you. (So you'll have eight words for each person, place, or event.)

5. Finally, examine what each of those crucial people, places, or events taught you about life.

   a. Was everything you learned positive?

b. Was everything you learned negative?

c. How do you make sense of having a mixed learning experience from each of those factors in your life?

d. What do you need to do to take the good and discard the bad teachings?

When I Felt Different

In this exercise, you will explore the experience of feeling excluded because you were or are different from other people in a group. The hope here is that by understanding your own experience of difference, you may come to understand the way other people feel when they are different from the majority.

1. On a sheet of paper, describe a time when you felt different from the rest of the people in a situation. What was the situation? Why did you feel different? How did you feel about yourself in that moment?

2. Discuss that experience with the other people in your group, or let your thoughts about that experience flow freely as you write on a fresh sheet of paper. Don't censor yourself, and don't judge yourself or others. Be as open as you can.

3. Now write down what you would say to yourself in that situation if you could go back. How would you encourage yourself? How would you help yourself understand the situation more fully?

4. Finally, discuss or journal through what you have come to understand about the experience of feeling different. What does your own experience teach you about how

others might feel when they are in the minority in a situation?

LEARNING THE HISTORY OF SLAVERY AND RACISM

The Time Line of Racism and Immigration

In this exercise, you will discover and recover what you have learned—and what you have not learned—about the history of racism and immigration in the United States. The hope here is that you will come to understand the long through line of racism and white supremacy in the United States and its legacy in twenty-first-century America.

1. Review a time line from Racial Equity Tools, found here: http://www.racialequitytools.org/resourcefiles/ racismimmigration-timeline.pdf.

2. Using three highlighters of different colors:

   a. Use one color to highlight historical facts that you knew fully.

   b. Use another color to highlight historical facts that you have heard of but didn't know the details about.

   c. Use the third color to highlight historical facts of which you were completely unaware.

3. In your group or in your journal, explore these questions:

   a. What historical facts did you know, and how did you come to know them?

   b. What historical facts did you misunderstand or not

understand in the context of the full history of racism and immigration?

c. What historical facts did you not know, and why do you think you didn't know them?

d. What does it say about your own personal knowledge and education to know certain things and not others? What responsibility do you have to further your own education and help others grow in their own knowledge about these topics?

Fear and Racism

In this exercise, you will be encouraged to examine how fear has historically influenced and shaped racist behaviors and how fear might influence your own behavior and attitudes today. The hope is that by openly addressing fear and its relation to racism, participants will begin to challenge their own fears about "others."

1. View the three-minute clip "A Brief History of the United States" (from the makers of *South Park* and originally part of the film *Bowling for Columbine*). You can find it on YouTube at https://www.youtube.com/watch?v=NPBHtjZmSpw.

2. Explore, either in group discussion or in your journal, the following questions:

a. What role did fear play, in your opinion, in the history of slavery and racism in the United States?

b. What role does fear play today in racism and white supremacy?

c. In what ways does fear affect how you view people of other races?

DISPELLING THE MYTHS AND APATHY AROUND SLAVERY AND RACISM

Get Over It!

In this exercise, you will explore the oft-stated idea that people should just "get over it" when it comes to issues of historical injustice and racism. The hope is that you will be able to both define what "it" is in these situations—whether "it" is something you think or something someone else says—and have ways to encourage dialogue around historical and contemporary racism.

1. Commit to yourself and/or the people with you that you will stay in the conversation even when it gets difficult.

2. Make a list of all the things people might mean by "it" when they say "Get over it." Consider:

   a. Historical events

   b. Personal experiences

   c. Emotions

3. Discuss or journal about what bothers you about the "its" on your list. Why are you bothered by these historical events, personal experiences, or emotions?

The Doll Experiment Re-created

In this exercise, you will be encouraged to understand racism as something systemic, something that invades every part of our society in the United States. The hope is that you will walk away understanding that racism is not something that just affects people from time to time but instead is a part of a lived reality that affects every aspect of the lives of people of color.

1. Watch the short film *Girl Like Me* by filmmaker Kiri Davis, available on YouTube at https://www.youtube.com/watch?v=YWyI77Yh1Gg.

2. Pay special heed to the section where Davis re-creates the "doll experiment" from the 1950s.

3. In your journal or with your group, consider these questions:

   a. What does the film show about the physical considerations that African American women must negotiate?

   b. What surprised you, if anything, about the doll experiment?

   c. How are people taught these standards of beauty and "goodness"? Where do we learn them?

   d. What things could you do to help break down these racist standards of beauty and self-worth?

EXAMINING THE IMAGERY OF GOD, JESUS, AND GOD'S KINGDOM IN OUR CHURCHES

A Visual Audit of Your Place of Worship and Your Home

In this exercise, you will identify the racial-ethnic identity of the people portrayed in the faith imagery of your home and church. The hope is that you will begin to see how pervasive white supremacy is in the imagery and visual representations of God, Jesus, and Christians in general.

1. Take a notebook and make a note about the racial or ethnic identity of any image of a person in your church and home. Consider these places:

   a. Stained glass windows

   b. Bulletins and church publications

   c. Paintings, sketches, murals, and drawings

   d. Images in Bibles

2. What patterns of race and ethnicity did you see? What percentage of the images were of white people? People of color? Did any images of Jesus show him as a man of Middle Eastern or African descent?

3. Discuss, in your journal or group, what your findings say about your church's or your family's concepts of the racial and ethnic makeup of God's kingdom.

4. If you feel that conception needs to change, what practical steps could you take to help shift the paradigm to include all the faces of God's kingdom?

Why Is Jesus a White Man? White Supremacy in Religious Films

In this exercise, you will be encouraged to become more aware of the racial and ethnic portrayal of religious figures in film. The hope is that you will come to a place where you challenge the portrayals of people of color by white actors when you see such occurrences in these films.

1. Make a list, either as a group or in your journal, of all the religious or religion-related films you know. Consider everything from *The Ten Commandments* to *When Calls the Heart*.

2. Use the Internet—IMDb is a good place to start—to make a list of all the people of color who have had a significant role in those films. Then make a list of the times when Jesus or his disciples are portrayed by people of color. Finally, make a list of all the times when Satan, Judas, or other figures of "evil" are portrayed by people of color.

3. In your group or your journal, discuss your findings. What do they suggest about the manifestation of white supremacy in film? What do they suggest about our concepts of God and Jesus? What do they suggest about our concept of evil as related to race?

STUDYING WHAT THE CHURCH HAS TAUGHT US ABOUT RACE AND ETHNICITY

Look to the Leaders
This exercise encourages you to consider who you look to for leadership in your faith, and the ethnic diversity that is or isn't present in the leaders you choose to guide you. The hope is that you will come to value ethnic diversity in your teachers of faith, if you don't already.

1. Make a list of all the people you look to for religious or spiritual teaching, such as the leaders in your church or

denomination, Christian authors or bloggers you read, online personalities, and television personalities.

2. How many of those people are white? How many are people of color? How many are men? How many are women?

3. Explore, in your group or in your journal, the following questions:

   a. What do you gain by being taught by people from various ethnicities and genders?

   b. What do you lose by being taught by only people who look like you?

   c. What can you do, if necessary, to diversify who teaches you?

Don't Be Bamboozled

This activity is designed to help you explore the way racist imagery and teaching pervades even the most seemingly innocuous parts of our lives. The hope is that you will come away from this experience with an increased knowledge that will help you spot and then dissect white supremacist and racist teaching when you see it.

1. Watch the film *Bamboozled* by Spike Lee.

2. In group discussion or your journal, explore your answers to the questions found online at https://www. slideshare .net/belair1981/bamboozled-spike-lee.

CHALLENGING WHITE SUPREMACY AND RECOGNIZING PRIVILEGE

What's in Your Knapsack?

In this exercise, you will be encouraged to recognize the ways in which you are privileged or underprivileged because of your ethnicity. The hope is that you will come to understand that these are things that you did not earn, and will thus begin to follow God's leading in the ways that you use your privilege to assist those who do not carry it.

1. Read the essay "White Privilege: Unpacking the Invisible Knapsack" by Peggy McIntosh with a pen or highlighter in hand. (Search for the essay online and you should be able to find it.)

2. Highlight or underline any examples of privilege that you think apply to you.

3. Make notes about other kinds of privilege because of your skin tone. Make notes about the way you suffer because of your skin tone.

4. In your journal or group, share your stories of when you have been privileged because of your ethnicity or persecuted because of your ethnicity.

5. Discuss ways in which you may use your white privilege, if you have it, to help "even the playing field." If you are a person of color, discuss ways in which you wish white people would recognize or use their privilege.

Drawing the Kingdom

In this exercise, you will prayerfully explore what the kingdom of God looks like from God's perspective. The hope is
that your God-given creativity will allow you to more fully
enter into God's vision for God's people.

1. Using whatever materials you'd like—paper, crayons,
   paint, clay, found objects, glitter—craft an image of what
   you imagine God's kingdom to be like in terms of God's
   people. Consider these questions:

   a. Who is there? What ethnicity are the people,
      specifically?

   b. What do the people there do?

   c. What does God's face—as best you can describe it—
      look like when looking at God's kingdom?

2. Discuss, in your journal or as a group, what you felt when
   you created an image of God's kingdom.

3. Then, consider what you see God doing in the part of
   God's kingdom in which you live to bring the kingdom
   more in line with God's dream.

Separating church and state

Is America a Christian Nation?

In this exercise, you are encouraged to explore what you
have been taught and what you believe about the religious
origins of the United States. The hope is that you will come
to a deeper and more complex understanding of our nation's
religious roots.

1. Read copies of the founding documents of the United States: the Declaration of Independence and the Constitution.

2. As you read, highlight any mentions of God and Jesus.

3. What do you see about Christian faith in those documents? What do you not see?

4. Why is it important for some people to consider America a Christian nation? What is the danger of that belief?

"What Is a Christian Nation?" Bingo: A Group Activity
This exercise will help you explore the myth of a Christian nation. The hope is that participants will come to a deeper understanding of the term *Christian*.

1. Create a bingo board of five spaces across and five down on the floor or on a large whiteboard. (Use a piece of paper if playing individually.)

2. Write the following terms on twenty-four small pieces of paper, then mix up the slips of paper in a hat or bowl:

> patriotism
> morality
> illegal abortion
> mercy
> centrality of family values
> exclusion
> a Christian president
> kindness
> majority of citizens identify as Christians
> public prayer

Christian founders

justice

national superiority

public display of the Ten Commandments

a strong military

forgiveness

integrity

focused on the less fortunate

illegal same-sex marriage

tolerance

an official state church

liberty

the right to bear arms

imperfection

3. Mark the center square of the board with a cross: that's your bonus square.

4. Now you're ready to play bingo! Draw one slip of paper at a time and place it anywhere you'd like on your board if it is part of the myth of a Christian nation. If it is not, simply set it aside.

5. When an individual or the group gets bingo (five in a row vertically, horizontally, or diagonally), create a list of all the terms that helped them win.

6. Discuss those terms. Do they define a Christian nation? Why or why not?

7. Finally, create a one- or two-sentence definition of a nation that operates on truly Christian principles.

SUBVERTING RACIST ECONOMIC SYSTEMS

Follow the Money

This exercise will help you see the long financial trail that slavery has left in our history. The hope is that participants will begin to consider the origins of our national and personal wealth.

1. Review these lists of companies and universities that have their roots in the American slave trade: go to the URLs http://atlantablackstar.com/2013/08/26/17-major-companies-never-knew-benefited-slavery/ and https://abagond.wordpress.com/2014/06/11/the-incomplete-list-of-us-companies-and-universities-that-benefited-from-black-slavery/.

2. With which, if any, of these companies do you have ties? How does this information make you feel about them? Does it change your willingness to be connected with them? Why or why not?

The Mosaic of Leaders

This exercise is designed to encourage you to understand the ethnic makeup of the leadership in organizations you support. The hope is that you will be challenged to make conscientious choices about where to spend your money, energy, and time.

1. Create a list, either in your journal or with your group, of ten organizations with which you are currently affiliated. These could be organizations in which you are an employee, customer, or volunteer; events that you attend;

or community organizations or coalitions of which you are a part.

2. Using the organizations' websites, look into the governing boards that guide these organizations. What percentage of their board is made up of people of color? If it's a conference, what percentage of the speakers are people of color?

3. How do you feel about the representation of people of color in these organizations? Does it affect how you think about the organization? Your work with them? Why or why not?

DISSECTING RACIAL AND ETHNIC ARCHETYPES AND STEREOTYPES

The Mosaic of Stereotypes: A Group Exercise

This exercise is designed to help you explore the racial and ethnic stereotypes you encounter. The hope is that you walk away with more ability to recognize those stereotypes and with more resolve to challenge them when you see them.

1. Look through various magazines and cut out any images of racial or ethnic stereotypes that appear in their pages. Use tape or sticky tack to hang them on a wall. Place the image against the wall so that no one can see the images.

2. Have one group member walk along the wall and turn over the images.

3. Study the images and journal about how you feel about them. What do you feel when you see those images? What makes you feel that way?

4. Discuss your feelings using these questions as a starting point:

   a. What emotions arose for you when you viewed those images?

   b. Which, if any, of these stereotypes have you thought to be true in some way?

   c. What jokes, slurs, or behavior assumptions are associated with these particular stereotypes?

   d. What are some ways you can help to challenge or break down these stereotypes? What are the challenges of doing so?

"I Don't Know Nothing" about Stereotypes

This exercise is designed to help you begin to recognize stereotypes when you see them. The hope is that by recognizing them, we can challenge them.

1. Watch one or more of the following clips from famous classic movies. (Note: this is just a small sample of available options.)

   a. *Gone with the Wind*: https://www.youtube.com/watch?v=PAV3OfHo4n4

   b. *Breakfast at Tiffany's*: https://www.youtube.com/watch?v=DC5RtcypOqE

   c. *Peter Pan*: https://www.youtube.com/watch?v=Y_at9dOElQk

   d. *Sixteen Candles*: https://www.youtube.com/watch?v=wc8e80qno_U

2. What stereotypes are portrayed in each sample? How do you feel about these portrayals? Can you recall how you felt when you first watched the films?

3. What is our responsibility when we see such stereotypes in film, TV, books, and so on?

RECOMMENDED BOOKS, FILMS, AND DOCUMENTARY SERIES

W E HAVE FOUND that reading and watching deeply in history and in contemporary books about racism, ethnocentrism, white privilege, and white supremacy is a profound way to open our minds and break our hearts for what breaks the heart of God.

Books

The New Jim Crow: Mass Incarceration in the Age of Colorblindness by Michelle Alexander

Slaves in the Family by Edward Ball

Slavery by Another Name: The Re-enslavement of Black Americans from the Civil War to World War II by Douglas A. Blackmon

The Color of Christ: The Son of God and the Saga of Race in America by Edward J. Blum and Paul Harvey

The Family Tree: A Lynching in Georgia, a Legacy of Secrets, and My Search for the Truth by Karen Branan

The Rightness of Whiteness: The World of a White Child in a Segregated Society by Abraham F. Citron

Between the World and Me by Ta-Nehisi Coates

Getting Jefferson Right: Fact-Checking Claims about Our Third President by Michael Coulter and Warren Throckmorton

Post-Traumatic Slave Syndrome: America's Legacy of Enduring Injury and Healing by Joy Angela DeGruy

Critical Race Theory: An Introduction by Richard Delgado and Jean Stefancic

Inheriting the Trade: A Northern Family Confronts Its Legacy as the Largest Slave-Trading Dynasty in U.S. History by Thomas Norman DeWolf

Gather at the Table: The Healing Journey of a Daughter of Slavery and a Son of the Slave Trade by Thomas Norman DeWolf and Sharon Leslie Morgan

The Color Line by Frederick Douglass

Narrative of the Life of Frederick Douglass by Frederick Douglass

At the Hands of Persons Unknown: The Lynching of Black America by Philip Dray

People of the Dream: Multiracial Congregations in the United States by Michael O. Emerson with Rodney M. Woo

The Negro American: A Documentary History by Leslie H. Fishel Jr. and Benjamin Quarles

How Starbucks Saved My Life: A Son of Privilege Learns to Live Like Everyone Else by Michael Gates Gill

Trouble I've Seen: Changing the Way the Church Views Racism by Drew G. I. Hart

Slavery and the Making of America by James Oliver Horton and Lois E. Horton

Jefferson's Children: The Story of One American Family by Shannon Lanier and Jane Feldman

Lies My Teacher Told Me: Everything Your American History Textbook Got Wrong by James W. Loewen

The Color of Wealth: The Story Behind the U.S. Racial Wealth Divide by Meizhu Lui, Barbara Robles, Betsy Leonder-Wright, Rose Brewer, and Rebecca Adamson

The House I Live In: Race in the American Century by Robert J. Norrell

Twelve Years a Slave by Solomon Northrup

More Than Equals: Racial Healing for the Sake of the Gospel by Spencer Perkins and Chris Rice

Us Plus Them: Tapping the Positive Power of Difference by Todd L. Pittinsky

Just Mercy: A Story of Justice and Redemption by Bryan Stevenson

Why Are All the Black Kids Sitting Together in the Cafeteria? And Other Conversations about Race by Beverly Daniel Tatum

Master of the Mountain: Thomas Jefferson and His Slaves by Henry Wiencek

The Warmth of Other Suns: The Epic Story of America's Great Migration by Isabel Wilkerson

Help Me to Find My People: The African American Search for Family Lost in Slavery by Heather Andrea Williams

Colorblind: The Rise of Post-Racial Politics and the Retreat from Racial Equality by Tim Wise

Dear White America: Letter to a New Minority by Tim Wise

White Like Me: Reflections on Race from a Privileged Son by Tim Wise

Films and documentary series

13th, directed by Ava DuVernay

The Birth of a Nation (2016), directed by Nate Parker

Eyes on the Prize: America's Civil Rights Years 1954–1965, produced by Henry Hampton

I Am Not Your Negro, directed by Raoul Peck

"The Difference Between Us," episode 1 of *Race: The Power of Illusion*, produced by Christine Herbes-Sommers

Reconstruction: The Second Civil War, directed by Llewellyn Smith

Traces of the Trade, directed by Katrina Browne, Alla Kovgan, and Jude Ray

NOTES

1 Where We Start: Introducing Plantation Jesus

1 *Slavery and the Making of America* (New York: Ambrose Video Pub., 2004).

2 Philip Dray, *At the Hands of Persons Unknown: The Lynching of Black America* (New York: Random House, 2002).

3 Tim Wise, "Racism 2.0 and the Burden of Blackness in the Age of Obama," *Tim Wise* (blog), September 15, 2012, http://www.timwise.org/2012/09/racism-2-0-and-the-burden-of-blackness-in-the-age-of-obama.

4 Beverly Daniel Tatum, *Why Are All the Black Kids Sitting Together in the Cafeteria? And Other Conversations about Race* (New York: Basic Books, 1997).

5 Frederick Douglass, *Narrative of the Life of Frederick Douglass, an American Slave* (Boston: Anti-Slavery Office, 1845), 118.

2 Why Can't We Talk? Ten Roadblocks to Real Conversation

1 Joy Angela DeGruy, *Post Traumatic Slave Syndrome: America's Legacy of Enduring Injury and Healing* (Milwaukie, OR: Uptone Press, 2005), 117.

2 Frederick Douglass, *Narrative of the Life of Frederick Douglass, an American Slave* (Boston: Anti-Slavery Office, 1845), 45.

3 James W. Loewen, *Lies My Teacher Told Me: Everything Your American History Textbook Got Wrong* (New York: Touchstone, 2007), 137. First edition published 1995.

4 Alexander Abad-Santos, "Paula Deen Has Lost Her Job," *The Atlantic*, June 21, 2013, https://www.theatlantic.com/national/archive/2013/06/paula-deen-today-show/314004/.

5 Fergus M. Bordewich, *Bound for Canaan* (New York: Harper Collins, 2005), 436–37.

6 "Slave Rebellions: A Timeline; Nat Turner: A Troublesome Property," *Independent Lens*, accessed August 28, 2015, http://www.pbs.org/independentlens/natturner/slave_rebellions.html.

7 Sharon Morgan, "400 Years a Slave," *Our Black Ancestry* (blog), November 9, 2013, https://ourblackancestry.wordpress.com/2013/11/09/400-years-a-slave/.

8 Po Bronson and Ashley Merryman, "Even Babies Discriminate: A NurtureShock Excerpt," *Newsweek*, September 4, 2009, http://www.newsweek.com/even-babies-discriminate-nurtureshock-excerpt-79233.

9 Martin Luther King Jr., "I Have a Dream" (address, 1963 March on Washington for Jobs and Freedom, Washington, D.C., August 28, 1963).

10 "Study: Nearly Half of Black Men Arrested by 23," TheGrio, last modified January 6, 2014, https://thegrio.com/2014/01/06/study-nearly-half-of-black-men-arrested-by-23/.

11 "Criminal Justice Fact Sheet," NAACP. org, accessed January 2, 2018. http://www.naacp.org/criminal-justice-fact-sheet/.

12 Signe-Mary McKernan, Caroline Ratcliffe, C. Eugene Steuerle, and Sisi Zhang, "Less Than Equal: Racial Disparities in Wealth Accumulation," Urban Institute, April 25, 2013, https://www.urban.org/research/publication/less-equal-racial-disparities-wealth-accumulation/view/full_report.

13 Peggy McIntosh, "White Privilege: Unpacking the Invisible
Knapsack," *Peace and Freedom Magazine*, July/August 1989,
10–12. The text of McIntosh's article is available on the website of
the National SEED Project at https://nationalseedproject.org/white
-privilege-unpacking-the-invisible-knapsack.

**3 How to Know What You Don't Know: The Face of Plantation
Jesus**

1 Dictionary.com, s.v. "ethnocentrism," accessed November 1,
2017, http://www.dictionary.com/browse/ethnocentrism?s=t.

2 "About *The Bible*," Outreach (website), accessed November 8,
2017, http://www.outreach.com/the-bible/about.aspx.

3 Wil Gafney, "Black Samson and White Women on the History
Channel," *Wil Gafney* (blog), April 11, 2013, http://www.wilgafney
.com/2013/03/11/black-samson-white-women-on-the-history
-channel/.

4 Wil Gafney, "What the History Channel Is Getting Wrong
about the Bible," *Huffington Post*, March 12, 2013, https://www
.huffingtonpost.com/rev-wil-gafney-phd/what-the-history
-channel-is-getting-wrong-about-the-bible_b_2854874.html.

5 Michael O. Emerson, "A New Day for Multiracial
Congregations," *Reflections*, Spring 2013, http://reflections.yale
.edu/article/future-race/new-day-multiracial-congregations.

6 Mike Fillon, "The Real Face of Jesus: Advances in Forensic
Science Reveal the Most Famous Face in History," *Popular
Mechanics*, December 2002, posted January 22, 2015, http://www
.popularmechanics.com/science/health/a234/1282186/.

7 Ibid.

8 Charles Honey, "Calvin College Art Gallery Exhibits Works
Known Well in Christian Homes," *Grand Rapids (MI) Press*,
January 11, 2003, B1.

9 Versions of this story can be found online (e.g., "Tim Wise
Addressing Race with His Daughters," posted March 25, 2011,
video, 7:08, https://www.youtube.com/watch?v=iHC3QiRKnwI)
and in Wise's book *White Like Me: Reflections on Race from a
Privileged Son*, rev. ed. (New York: Soft Skull Press, 2011), 317–22.

10 James H. Cone, *The Cross and the Lynching Tree* (Maryknoll, NY: Orbis Books, 2013).

11 Matthew C. Ogilvie, "Children of a White God: A Study of Racist 'Christian' Theologies," *Human Nature Review* 1 (2001): 1–27, http://human-nature.com/nibbs/01/ogilvie.html.

12 Michael O. Emerson with Rodney M. Woo, *People of the Dream: Multiracial Congregations in the United States* (Princeton, NJ: Princeton University Press, 2008), 149.

13 Abraham F. Citron, *The Rightness of Whiteness: The World of the White Child in a Segregated Society* (Detroit: Michigan-Ohio Regional Educational Laboratory, 1969).

14 Miles Willis, "The Passion of the Whites," The Black Commentator, last modified March 11, 2004, http://www.blackcommentator.com/81/81_think_piece_jesus.html.

15 Edward J. Blum and Paul Harvey, *The Color of Christ: The Son of God and the Saga of Race in America* (Chapel Hill: University of North Carolina Press, 2014).

4 What to Believe: Reading the Bible on the Plantation

1 Desmond Tutu, *No Future without Forgiveness* (New York: Penguin Random House, 2000), 31.

2 For more on ways to faithfully interpret these passages that have been used to support slavery, see Dennis R. Edwards, *1 Peter*, Story of God Bible Commentary (Grand Rapids, MI: Zondervan, 2017); Brian K. Blount et al., *True to Our Native Land: An African American New Testament Commentary* (Minneapolis: Fortress Press, 2007); Emerson B. Powery and Rodney S. Sadler Jr., *The Genesis of Liberation: Biblical Interpretation in the Antebellum Narratives of the Enslaved* (Nashville: Westminster John Knox Press, 2016); Willard M. Swartley, *Slavery, Sabbath, War, and Women: Case Studies in Biblical Interpretation* (Scottdale, PA: Herald Press, 1983); and James H. Cone, *The Cross and the Lynching Tree* (Maryknoll, NY: Orbis Books, 2013).

3 Leslie H. Fishel and Benjamin Quarles, *The Negro American: A Documentary History* (Glenview, IL: Scott Foresman, 1967), 114.

4 Palmer Becker, *Anabaptist Essentials: Ten Signs of a Unique Christian Faith* (Harrisonburg, VA: Herald Press, 2017), 49.

5 Acton Institute, "How Did Christian Slave Owners Justify Slavery?," featuring Susan Wise Bauer, posted October 20, 2008, video, 1:45, https://www.youtube.com/watch?v= rDV1e1yPpk0&feature=youtu.be.

6 "Philemon's Relationship to Onesimus," in *Philemon*, IVP New Testament Commentary Series, Bible Gateway, accessed December 17, 2017, https://www.biblegateway.com/resources/commentaries/ IVP-NT/Phlm/Philemons-Relationship.

7 Miles Willis, "The Passion of the Whites," The Black Commentator, last modified March 11, 2004, http://www .blackcommentator.com/81/81_think_piece_jesus.html.

8 "Pastors Conference for 'White Christians' Underway," WAFF 48 News, last modified July 4, 2012, http://www.waff .com/story/18952777/pastors-conference-for-white-christians -underway.

9 Alan Collins, "Winfield Residents Upset over Flier for Whites Only Pastors Conference," 14 News, last modified July 3, 2012, http://www.14news.com/story/18944454/winfield-residents-upset -over-flier-for-whites-only-pastors-conference.

5 Who's Got the Power? White Supremacy Doesn't Just Wear Hoods

1 Richard Delgado and Jean Stefancic, *Critical Race Theory: An Introduction* (New York: New York University Press, 2001).

2 Peggy McIntosh, "White Privilege: Unpacking the Invisible Knapsack," *Peace and Freedom Magazine*, July/August 1989, 10–12.

3 Tim Wise, "F.A.Q.s.," Tim Wise (website), last modified December 2014, accessed August 27, 2015, http://www.timwise .org/f-a-q-s/.

4 Ashley Nellis, "The Color of Justice: Racial and Ethnic Disparity in State Prisons," The Sentencing Project, last modified June 14, 2016, http://www.sentencingproject.org/publications/color-of -justice-racial-and-ethnic-disparity-in-state-prisons/.

5   Dayna Bowen Matthew, Edward Rodrigue, and Richard V. Reeves, "Time for Justice: Tackling Race Inequalities in Health and Housing," Brookings Institution, last modified October 19, 2016, https://www.brookings.edu/research/time-for-justice-tackling -race-inequalities-in-health-and-housing/.

6   Fergus M. Bordewich, "Monticello's Slave-Driver," *Wall Street Journal*, November 1, 2012, https://www.wsj.com/articles/ SB10001424052970203880704578087510516735272.

7   Henry Wiencek, *Master of the Mountain: Thomas Jefferson and His Slaves* (New York: Farrar, Straus and Giroux, 2012).

8   Bordewich, "Monticello's Slave-Driver."

9   David Barton, *The Jefferson Lies: Exposing the Myths You've Always Believed about Thomas Jefferson* (Nashville: Thomas Nelson, 2012).

10 See, for example, Warren Throckmorton and Michael L. Coulter, *Getting Jefferson Right: Fact Checking Claims about Our Third President* (Grove City, PA: Salem Grove Press, 2012).

11 Elise Hu, "Publisher Pulls Controversial Thomas Jefferson Book, Citing Loss of Confidence," National Public Radio, August 9, 2012, http://www.npr.org/sections/thetwo-way/2012/ 08/09/158510648/publisher-pulls-controversial-thomas-jefferson -book-citing-loss-of-confidence.

12 John Fea, "What Can We Learn from the David Barton Controversy?" *The Anxious Bench* (blog), Patheos, August 15, 2012, http://www.patheos.com/blogs/anxiousbench/2012/08/ what-can-we-learn-from-the-david-barton-controversy/.

13 Frederick Douglass, "The Meaning of July Fourth for the Negro," in *The Life and Writings of Frederick Douglass*, ed. Philip S. Foner, vol. 2, *Pre–Civil War Decade 1850–1860* (New York: International Publishers, 1950). Text available at Africans in America (website), http://www.pbs.org/wgbh/aia/part4/4h2927t.html.

14 United States Supreme Court, Roger Brooke Taney, John H. Van Evrie, and Samuel A. Cartwright, *The Dred Scott Decision: Opinion of Chief Justice Taney* (New York: Van Evrie, Horton, and Co., 1860), 19, retrieved from the Library of Congress, https:// www.loc.gov/item/17001543/.

15 Economic Policy Institute, "Poverty," *The State of Working America*, accessed November 7, 2017, http://stateofworkingamerica .org/fact-sheets/poverty/.

16 "Labor Force Statistics from the Current Population Survey: E-16. Unemployment Rates by Age, Sex, Race, and Hispanic or Latino Ethnicity," Bureau of Labor Statistics, accessed November 7, 2017, https://www.bls.gov/web/empsit/cpsee_e16.htm.

17 Tim J. Wise, *Colorblind: The Rise of Post-Racial Politics and the Retreat from Racial Equity* (San Francisco: City Lights Books, 2010).

18 Wende Marshall, "White Supremacy and Mass Incarceration," Al Jazeera English, last modified January 22, 2013, http://www .aljazeera.com/indepth/opinion/2013/01/201311782939161836 .html%22.

19 Associated Press, "Racial Disparities Persist in Higher-Paying Jobs," NBC News, last modified April 28, 2009, http://www .nbcnews.com/id/30437468#Vd9mlHvYfn4.

20 James W. Loewen, *Lies My Teacher Told Me: Everything Your American History Textbook Got Wrong* (New York: New Press, 2007), 143.

21 Ibid., 144.

22 Michael O. Emerson with Rodney M. Woo, *People of the Dream: Multiracial Congregations in the United States* (Princeton, NJ: Princeton University Press, 2008), 42–44.

6 Who We Worship: The Myth of America as a Christian Nation

1 Richard Fausset, "As Trump Rises, So Do Some Hands Waving Confederate Battle Flags," *New York Times*, November 18, 2016, https://www.nytimes.com/2016/11/19/us/confederate-flag-trump .html.

2 Stanley Hauerwas, "Christians, Don't Be Fooled: Trump Has Deep Religious Convictions," *Washington Post*, January 27, 2017, https://www.washingtonpost.com/news/acts-of-faith/wp/2017/ 01/27/christians-dont-be-fooled-trump-has-deep-religious -convictions/?utm_term=.e6021162feca.

3 Billy Graham, "What Is Your Definition of a Christian?" Billy Graham Evangelistic Association, last modified March 4, 2010, https://billygraham.org/answer/what-is-your-definition-of-a-christian-if-someone-were-to-ask-them-most-of-my-friends-would-say-they-are-christians-and-most-of-them-go-to-church-at-least-occasionally-but-im-not-sure-they-rea/.

4 Heather Andrea Williams, *Help Me to Find My People: The African American Search for Family Lost in Slavery* (Chapel Hill: University of North Carolina Press, 2012), 90.

5 Ibid., 2.

6 Ibid, 3.

7 "Traces of the Trade: A Story from the Deep North: Film Description," PBS, accessed December 12, 2017, http://www.pbs.org/pov/tracesofthetrade/film-description/.

8 *Traces of the Trade*, directed by Katrina Browne (Washington, D.C.: Ebb Pod Productions, 2008).

9 *The Week* staff, "Did the Founding Fathers Really Work 'Tirelessly' to End Slavery?" *The Week*, June 30, 2011, http://theweek.com/articles/483581/did-founding-fathers-really-work-tirelessly-end-slavery.

10 *The Abolitionists*, directed by Rob Rapley, American Experience, aired January 8, 2013, on PBS.

7 Where Is the Money? Plantation Economics Today

1 *The Fab Five*, directed by Jason Hehir (Bristol, CT: ESPN Films, 2011).

2 Frederick Douglass, "'The Color Line'" *The North American Review*, June, 1881," in *Frederick Douglass: Selected Speeches and Writings* (Chicago: Lawrence Hill, 1999), 653.

3 John Henrik Clarke, "Race: An Evolving Issue in Western Thought," *Journal of Human Relations* 18, no. 3 (1970), 1042–54. Text available at http://www.nbufront.org/MastersMuseums/JHClarke/ArticlesEssays/RaceInWesternThought.html.

4 Samuel H. Williamson and Louis P. Cain, "Measuring Slavery in 2016 Dollars," MeasuringWorth, accessed December 13, 2017,

http://www.measuringworth.com/slavery.php.

5 Thomas Jefferson to John Holmes, April 22, 1820, Thomas
Jefferson Papers, Series 1: General Correspondence, 1651–1827,
Library of Congress, Washington, D.C., https://www.loc.gov/item/
mtjbib023795/.

6 Marybeth Gasman, "Fighting for the Future of Black Men:
Southern University's Role," *Huffington Post*, August 29, 2012,
http://www.huffingtonpost.com/marybeth-gasman/hbcus-and
-black-men_b_1831951.html, italics added.

7 Sven Beckert and Seth Rockman, "How Slavery Led to Modern
Capitalism," *Huffington Post*, February 24, 2014, http://www
.huffingtonpost.com/2014/02/24/slavery_n_4847105.html.

8 *Atlanta Black Star* staff, "15 Major Corporations You Never
Knew Profited from Slavery," *Atlanta Black Star*, August 26, 2013,
http://atlantablackstar.com/2013/08/26/17-major-companies
-never-knew-benefited-slavery/.

9 "CBS Sports, Turner Broadcasting, NCAA Reach 14-Year
Agreement," NCAA, last modified January 12, 2011, http://www
.ncaa.com/news/basketball-men/2010-04-21/cbs-sports-turner
-broadcasting-ncaa-reach-14-year-agreement.

10 *Frontline*, season 29, episode 10, "Money and March Madness,"
produced by Zachary Stauffer, featuring Lowell Bergman, aired
March 29, 2011, on PBS, https://www.pbs.org/wgbh/frontline/
film/money-and-march-madness/. Transcript available at https://
www.pbs.org/wgbh/pages/frontline/money-and-march-madness/
etc/transcript.html.

11 National Collegiate Athletic Association, *1999–00–2009–10
NCAA Student-Athlete Race and Ethnicity Report*, comp. Erin
Zgonc (Indianapolis: NCAA, 2010), http://www.ncaapublications
.com/productdownloads/SAEREP11.pdf.

12 "Sports Sponsorship, Participation, and Demographics Search,"
NCAA.com, accessed January 2, 2017, http://web1.ncaa.org/
rgdSearch/exec/displayResultsPercents.

13 "Average Athletic Scholarship per Varsity Athlete,"
Scholarshipstats, accessed September 12, 2017, http://www
.scholarshipstats.com/average-per-athlete.html.

14 Cork Gaines, "The Difference in How Much Money Schools Make off of College Sports Is Jarring, and It Is the Biggest Obstacle to Paying Athletes," Business Insider, October 14, 2016, http://www.businessinsider.com/ncaa-schools-college-sports-revenue-2016-10.

15 Ibid.

16 Michael Lewis, "Serfs of the Turf," New York Times, November 11, 2007, http://www.nytimes.com/2007/11/11/opinion/11lewis.html.

17 "Bilas Calls NCAA System 'Profoundly Immoral,'" interview by Dennis Berman, Wall Street Journal, March 15, 2013, video, 5:22, http://www.wsj.com/video/bilas-calls-ncaa-system-profoundly-immoral/01F65809-46F7-4881-8DEF-4EAF7B14997D.html.

18 Jesse Reed, "Chris Webber Says NCAA Must Change: It's Slavery Now," Fox Sports, August 18, 2015, http://www.foxsports.com/college-football/story/chris-webber-says-ncaa-must-change-it-s-slavery-now-081815.

19 The Center for Law and Justice, "New Jim Crow Fact Sheet," accessed November 8, 2017, http://www.cflj.org/programs/new-jim-crow/new-jim-crow-fact-sheet/.

20 Eric Markowitz, "Making Profits on the Captive Prison Market," New Yorker, September 4, 2016, https://www.newyorker.com/business/currency/making-profits-on-the-captive-prison-market.

21 U.S. Department of Education, Policy and Programs Study Service, State and Local Expenditures on Corrections and Education, July 2016, https://www2.ed.gov/rschstat/eval/other/expenditures-corrections-education/brief.pdf.

22 Michelle Alexander, The New Jim Crow: Mass Incarceration in the Age of Colorblindness (New York: The New Press, 2012), 4.

8 Where Do We Go from Here? Following the Real Jesus

1 Martin Luther King Jr., "Where Do We Go from Here?" (speech, 11th annual SCLC Convention, Atlanta, GA, August 16, 1967), http://kingencyclopedia.stanford.edu/encyclopedia/documentsentry/where_do_we_go_from_here_delivered_at_the_11th_annual_sclc_convention/.

2 "About Us," Stones Church, accessed December 13, 2017, http://
stoneschurch.com/about/.

3 Theresa Cho, personal communication with authors,
September 9, 2017.

4 Sean Hamon, personal communication with authors,
September 11, 2017.

5 Ibid.

6 Brian Cordova, personal communication with authors,
September 9, 2017.

7 Peggy Mumper, personal communication with authors,
September 10, 2017.

8 Lia Scholl, personal communication with authors, September
12, 2017.

9 "COB Statement RE: Violence in Charlottesville, Virginia,"
African Methodist Episcopal Church, last modified August 14,
2017, https://www.ame-church.com/news/cob-statement-re
-violence-charlottesville-virginia/.

10 "Who We Are," Progressive National Baptist Convention Inc.,
accessed October 16, 2017, http://www.pnbc.org/Who-We-Are.

11 "Racial Righteousness," The Evangelical Covenant Church,
accessed October 16, 2017, http://www.covchurch.org/justice/
racial-righteousness/sankofa/.

12 "Intercultural Development," The Evangelical Covenant
Church, accessed October 16, 2017, http://www.covchurch.org/
justice/intercultural-development/.

13 "What Is Arrabon?" Arrabon, accessed November 8, 2017,
http://www.arrabon.com/.

14 Hamon, personal communication.

15 Ibid.

16 Peggy Mumper, personal communication with authors,
September 12, 2017.

17 *Washington Post* staff, "Transcript: Obama Delivers Eulogy for
Charleston Pastor, the Rev. Clementa Pinckney," *Washington Post*,
June 26, 2015, https://www.washingtonpost.com/news/post
-nation/wp/2015/06/26/transcript-obama-delivers-eulogy

-for-charleston-pastor-the-rev-clementa-pinckney/?utm_
term=.23fc86dab015.

Resources and Exercises

1 "Vision, Mission, Approach, Values, and Facebook Community
Guideline," Coming to the Table, accessed January 2, 2018. http://
comingtothetable.org/about-us/vision-mission-values/.

The Authors

Skot Welch is the principal/founder of Global Bridge-builders, a firm focusing on cultural transformation and inclusion that serves a wide range of clients in the United States and in more than seven countries. Welch has worked in international business and diversity and inclusion management for nearly twenty years. Welch  received a bachelor's degree from Albion College and a master's degree in management and international marketing from Aquinas College. He and his wife, Barbara, have two children.

Rick Wilson was an Emmy-winning producer and writer in print and broadcast media. He was cohost, with Skot Welch, of the popular radio program *Radio in Black and White*, which covered topics related to race, ethnicity, and cultural competence. Wilson died in 2014 and is survived by his wife, Laurie; five children; and four grandchildren.

Andi Cumbo-Floyd is a writer, editor, and writing coach whose books include *The Slaves Have Names*, a book of creative nonfiction that tells the story of the people who were enslaved on the plantation that she calls home.
 She holds a master of fine arts in creative nonfiction from Antioch University, a master of arts in literature from Case Western Reserve University, and a bachelor of arts in English and history from Messiah College. She and her husband, Philip, run a small farm in central Virginia.

CPSIA information can be obtained
at www.ICGtesting.com
Printed in the USA
BVHW04*0737180518
516569BV00011B/11/P

9 781513 803319